Reliant Scimitar

Elvis Payne

NOSTALGIA ROAD

First published by Crécy Publishing Ltd 2018

A CIP record for this book is available from the British Library

ISBN 9781908347473

Printed in Bulgaria by MultiPrint

**Nostalgia Road is an imprint of
Crécy Publishing Limited**
1a Ringway Trading Estate
Shadowmoss Road
Manchester M22 5LH
www.crecy.co.uk

All images are from author's collection unless otherwise stated. All images marked RSSOC are from the Reliant Sabre & Scimitar Owners Club.

Front main:
A striking pose of a 1966 Scimitar GT. Worth noting is the position of the number plate, Reliant stated it was styled into the car at a position that could help direct fresh air into the engine compartment to assist cooling. *Thomas Touw*

Right inset:
Fitted with 1420 H show plates, this particular Scimitar GTE is believed to be one of Princess Anne's former Scimitars. *Dave Poole*

Left inset:
While the Sabre had been predominantly an open-top vehicle, the Sabre Six was the opposite, with almost all cars having a fixed top; only two open-top Sixes were manufactured.

Back cover main right:
With the 1,300cc engine being phased out by Ford in late 1986, the 1300 model was replaced with the Scimitar SS1 1400 in 1987. *Dave Poole*

Back cover main left:
Like earlier Scimitars, the SE6 enjoyed healthy exports all over the world. This particular vehicle was pictured near Swan River in Perth, Western Australia. *Neil Corfe*

Back cover inset clockwise from top left:
The main body panels of the Scimitar SS1 consisted of a number of processes and materials. *Paul Willetts*

Based on an original Scimitar GTE chassis, the 4x4 chassis was developed by Reliant in 1973, although it remained a one-off. *Dave Poole*

Neither the Sabre nor Sabre Six went into rallying half-heartedly and were often pushed to the max. *John Valler*

Artwork concept for the FW8 based on a redesigned Bond Equipe. *Martin North*

More than 50 years later, Sabre Six 660 XYB can still be found on the track, as seen here at Curborough Sprint Course in 2017. *Dave Poole*

With chassis number 003, this particular vehicle is classed as the first true Scimitar GT to be built. *Matt Greenly*

Back flap: Elvis Payne. *Harvey Payne*

CONTENTS

HRH The Princess Royal with her current 1989 Middlebridge Scimitar GTE. *Mick Gaughran*

Foreword by
HRH The Princess Royal

The Reliant Scimitar GTE has always been a car that I have much admired. When launched it was quite unique and I was fortunate to receive my first Scimitar GTE in 1970. It was aircraft blue with a light grey interior trim and fitted with alloy wheels. Over the following years I went on to own a number of Reliant Scimitar GTEs and currently still own a Middlebridge Scimitar.

I am pleased that Mr Payne has taken the time and effort to write this book, which is the second in the series concentrating on the Reliant Motor Company. The virtues of the Reliant Scimitar in particular are much underrated and I am sure this book will give a lot of pleasure to both past and present Reliant owners, detailing as it does the company's sports car history.

BUCKINGHAM PALACE

The author's wife, Caroline, and seven-year-old son Harvey in a 1965 Reliant Scimitar GT owned by Martin North.

Introduction

Few would have believed that when a small engineering company started producing three-wheeled vans in 1935 it would go on to produce a sports car that would be emulated in one form or another by almost every other car manufacturer around the world. The company was of course the Reliant Engineering Company (Tamworth) Ltd (as it was originally known), whose three-wheeled vehicles help the company to thrive, even at times when many other similar manufacturers fell by the wayside.

With the three-wheelers as the company's main 'bread and butter', Reliant's co-founder and Managing Director, Tom Williams, initially had no interest in manufacturing a four-wheeler. As a result, he dismissed any notions of building one. It was demand for a competitive four-wheeled vehicle in Israel that made Williams rethink the idea, although it was not until Ray Wiggin joined the company in 1959 that things really took off. Before long, his drive and enthusiasm was pushing the company upwards, leading Reliant into the sports car market with the introduction of a Sabra, Sabre and then a Scimitar GT.

Upon its introduction this next model would break the mould, as it went against all the conventional practices for a sports car of that era. The Scimitar GTE was something the world had never seen before, a car that was both a sports car and an estate rolled into one. Approving such a design was an ambitious and indeed brave decision by Wiggin. With its unique rising waistline styled by Ogle Design Ltd, it looked like nothing else on the road. Suddenly people didn't have to choose whether to purchase a sports car or a family estate car; with the Scimitar GTE they could have both. For many, it really was an eye-opener. Not only did the Scimitar GTE have good looks, but with its powerful engines it also had the performance to

match, together with fairly decent fuel economy. It soon became a phenomenon in its own right and an instant hit with a number of celebrities and Royals.

While it became a huge success for Reliant, the world continued to turn and its competition continued to improve and change with the times. For the Scimitar GTE, however, a change of management at Reliant in 1977 halted all future development. As sales started to decrease and the general public demanded more economical vehicles, Reliant adopted a new approach with a new small sports car, starting with the launch of the Scimitar SS1 in 1985. This was redeveloped throughout the 1980s and early 1990s, although despite its highs and lows nothing captured the success that had been enjoyed by the Scimitar GTE.

Reliant made numerous vehicles – three-wheelers, economy four-wheelers, sports cars – and developed motor industries in Israel and Turkey. However, many people only ever associate the company with its three-wheelers (especially the Reliant Robin) and thus remain completely unaware that Reliant also built ground-breaking sports cars. The scope of this book is to cover Reliant's involvement with sports cars only and the vehicles that led up to its creation, so it only details those parts of Reliant's history that affect those models. A more in-depth overview of the history of Reliant, the vehicles it manufactured and its various projects, can be found in the companion book *The Reliant Motor Company* by the same author, which also includes a foreword from HRH The Princess Royal.

As always, I would like to thank my wife Caroline and my son Harvey for the continued support they provide. Harvey really wanted to help with this book, so took some of the photos used in it.

5

An unknown sporting Reliant pick-up concept from the Ogle Design studios. *Peter Stevens*

Acknowledgements

First of all I would like to express my gratitude to HRH The Princess Royal for agreeing to provide a foreword for this book. Special thanks should also go to Barrie Wills, Dave Poole and Tom Karen; it is their tireless dedication and knowledge that has helped to inspire me and made this book possible.

Thanks should also go to: Andy Plumb, Anne Sullivan, *Autocar*, Barry Mansfield-Stokes, Barry Sidwells, Carl Langridge, Charlotte Oliver, Dave Allen, Dave Corby, David Louch, Derrick Smith, Ed Osmond, Freddy McGowan, Gautam Sem, Giles Chapman Library, Gill Richardson (and everyone at Crécy Publishing), Graham Hodgson, Graham Walker Ltd, Guy Belts, Harvey Payne, John Valler, John Hawthorn, Jonathan Heynes, Kerry Croxton, Marcello Gandini, Mark Cropper, Martin North, Matt Greenly, Mick Gaughran, Neil Corfe, Onur Selçuk, Pat Afford (acknowledging Ewart Thompson and Colin Fine-Thompson), Paul Willets, Peter Stevens, Philip Andrew, Reliant Motor Club, Reliant PartsWorld, Reliant Sabre & Scimitar Owners Club, Ritchie Spencer, Roger Gut, Ruth Kitchen (acknowledging Ray Wiggin), Steve Cropley, Stewart Halstead, Thomas Touw, Tony Heath, Tony Stafford, and Xavier de la Chapelle.

Reliant co-founder Tom Williams with a model of Reliant's first four-wheeled passenger car, the Carmel (designed for the Israeli market), behind him.

Reliant co-founder Ewart Thompson. Unlike Williams, who passed away in 1964, he lived to see the company start from nothing and reach the pinnacle of its success in the 1970s.

From tricycles to sports cars

The beginnings

The roots of the Scimitar can be traced right back to 1934 when a Mr Tom L. Williams left the Raleigh bicycle company in Nottingham, where he had been the Chief Designer for its three-wheeled vans, and, together with Ewart S. ('Tommo') Thompson, started to build the first Reliant prototype in his back garden at 'Bro-Dawel' in Tamworth. A year later the Reliant Engineering Company (Tamworth) Ltd was founded. Initially the three-wheeled vans it built were powered by J.A.P. engines, but these were soon replaced in 1938 with a power unit from the Austin 7. When, shortly afterwards, Austin announced that it was to cease manufacture of the engine, Reliant set about building its own version, which was completed in September 1939. As with all other motor manufacturers, Reliant stopped producing vehicles during the Second World War and instead turned its hand to manufacturing parts for the various ministries as part of the war effort.

'Bro-Dawel' on the Kettlebrook Road in Tamworth, where the first Reliant prototype was built in 1934. The house was awarded a blue plaque in July 2017.

The blue plaque at 'Bro-Dawel' awarded by the Reliant Motor Club and Tamworth Heritage Trust.

TAMWORTH HERITAGE TRUST

The first
Reliant 3-wheeled van
was built here in 1934
by
T. L. Williams and
E. S. Thompson.
It was registered on
January 1st 1935.

RELIANT MOTOR CLUB

Following the war, production of the three-wheeled vans recommenced in 1946, although most were destined for the export market, with home orders having to wait several weeks before taking delivery. At this point Reliant was fairly content with its products and had no intentions whatsoever of building a vehicle with four wheels. Indeed, a 1950 Reliant publication states that Tom Williams was asked many times, 'Why don't you make a four-wheeler?' to which he replied:

'Why should we? The three-wheeler has decided advantages over the four-wheeler, the myth that it easily turns over has been exploded. I could turn a four-wheeler over if I wished.'

In the same year Reliant introduced its Regent three-wheeled van with a 10cwt payload. This offered a more up-to-date version of its earlier vans, although it was still powered by the original 747cc side-valve Reliant engine.

The first Reliant prototype is seen here in 1935 with Ewart Thompson at the wheel, with his two-year-old daughter Pat. *Pat Afford*

The 10cwt Reliant Regent prototype in 1950, with Ewart Thompson in the driver's seat. *Pat Afford*

The south side of the Reliant premises on the A5 in Tamworth, a view that remained virtually unchanged for several decades.

A 1953 Reliant Regal. This was Reliant's first three-wheeled passenger car capable of carrying a family of four, and as a result it became very successful.

By 1953 Reliant had introduced its first passenger car, the three-wheeled Reliant Regal, which now featured an open body (still made of metal) with four seats and a foldaway hood. As the Regal could be driven on a motorcycle licence, for many motorcyclists with families it was the idea family car, especially when compared with a motorcycle and sidecar combination. Still powered by the 747cc Reliant engine, it was also more car-like than other three-wheelers, which tended to use smaller motorcycle engines. The Regal continued to evolve and 1956 saw the introduction of the Reliant Regal Mk III, which by then featured a complete fibreglass body. Constantly refining the Regal and moving forward with newer models made it a great success and allowed Reliant to expand rapidly. Then, several years later, just as it seemed that Reliant would only ever make three-wheelers, something changed.

The foundations of a sports car

Reliant had always benefited from a healthy market in export orders, with some dating back to pre-Reliant times through the fulfilment of outstanding orders after Raleigh ceased manufacturing its Light Delivery Van (LDV). Reliant had been successfully exporting the Regent 10cwt three-wheeler to Israel for a number of years, initially to a manufacturer called Schneller, before his business was sold to Yitzhak Shubinsky, a shipper and import merchant. Shubinsky continued to build the business, buying Regents from Reliant in a semi-knocked-down (SKD) format, although, unlike in the UK, three-wheelers in Israel did not benefit from cheaper tax brackets. As a result three-wheelers were in direct competition with four-wheeled vehicles from larger manufacturers. Shubinsky therefore believed that a four-wheeler was needed, and he suggested to Tom Williams that if Reliant manufactured one it would have a much better marketing advantage.

Although Williams was pretty adamant that Reliant did not need to build a four-wheeler, he was very astute and understood the point Shubinsky was making. He therefore agreed that Reliant should go ahead and develop one. Known initially as the Regent Four, the vehicle was designed as a utility four-wheeler that was robust enough to survive the pounding from Israel's rough roads. Shubinsky had also insisted that the vehicle should carry a 10cwt payload at 50mph (80km/h) and could be manufactured in a number of styles offering saloon, station wagon (estate), van and pick-up variations.

Reliant responded to the challenge and created its first chassis for a four-wheeler, which bore many similarities to the standard three-wheeler chassis with flanged box-section main members and tubular cross-bracing members. However, unlike the three-wheeler chassis,

Although the Reliant Regal Mk III was the first all-fibreglass passenger vehicle, the first all-fibreglass van came in the form of a Regal Mk IV with double doors at the back.

it used 16-gauge steel, making it both stronger and heavier. Very early on it was recognised that the Reliant 747cc side-valve engine did not have sufficient power for the Regent Four, so Reliant turned to Ford, and used that company's 1,172cc water-cooled side-valve engine, as fitted to the Ford Popular. Producing 36bhp at 4,400rpm, this then drove the rear axle via a three-speed synchromesh gearbox (also from the Ford Popular) and a needle-jointed propeller shaft.

With Reliant working on what it knew well, it was of little surprise that the body of the Regent Four shared features with the three-wheeled Reliant Regal Mk IV van that was in production at that time. Like the Regal, the Regent Four used a fibreglass body bonded to an ash frame, although it was much longer at 12ft 2in (3.7 metres), compared with the 10ft 8in (3.2 metres) of the Regal Mk IV, and had a modified wider front end to house both wheels.

The first batch of Regent Four four-wheelers was shipped to Autocars Ltd in Israel on 12 April 1958 as complete knock-down (CKD) kits together with components for a prototype fibreglass body, so that bodies could be made locally in Israel. While the chassis and initial body moulds were supplied by Reliant, the engines and gearboxes were sent directly from Ford as complete units. The vehicles would then be assembled in both Haifa and Tel Aviv, and as such the Regent Four is believed to have been an export model only.

This was effectively Reliant's first brochure to show a four-wheeler in 1958, with the Regent Four 10cwt van alongside the three-wheeled Regal Mk IV 5cwt van.

While Reliant's first four-wheeled vehicle, the Regent Four, featured a completely new chassis, its body had more than a passing similarity to that of the three-wheeled Regal Mk IV van.

As with the body, the chassis of the Regent Four bore similarities to that of its three-wheeled ancestors. Also note the steering wheel on the left-hand side, signifying that this was intended as an export model.

Above: Reliant displayed its first four-wheeler, the Regent Four, at the Commercial Motor Transport Exhibition at Earls Court, London, in 1958.

Left: The Regent Four continued to be developed heavily for the Israeli market, and was renamed the Sussita. It became most popular in this pick-up version. *Thomas Touw*

Once production was under way in Israel, the model name was changed from Regent Four to Sussita. More than 6,000 kits were sent from Reliant to Israel within the first five years. The vehicle continued to change, with a number of modifications including changes to the body styling, then in 1962 the engine was switched to a 997cc Ford Anglia 105E unit, which offered an extra 3bhp. The Sussita was also briefly sold in the USA and Canada as the Sabra. Sabra being the fruit of a local-growing cactus native to the Haifa region, and also the term for a native-born Israeli Jew, so was a particularly symbolic choice. Despite a positive reception at the 1960 New York Trade Fair, it is believed that fewer than 150 vehicles were actually exported.

With the success of the Sussita, Shubinsky believed that the people of Israel also needed a modern family car. This time he requested Reliant to design and engineer a new family car (codenamed FW3), which came to be called the Carmel (a mountain that overlooks Haifa). As with the Regent Four, the new car shared a similar styling with Reliant's three-wheeler range, which at that time was the Regal 3/25 saloon. The Carmel had a two-door fibreglass body that, like the Regal 3/25, incorporated a Ford Anglia-style reverse slant window. Powered by a 1,198cc engine from a Ford Anglia Super, producing 47bhp, the car also featured a suspension system that could deal with some of the rough roads in Israel, with independent suspension all round using swing axles at the rear and combined coil springs and dampers at the front. Once production started, it was soon realised that the reverse slant rear window was not being well received, so within a year the moulds were changed to create a more traditional style for the rear window.

Above right: The Carmel prototype being tested outside the Works Engineers Department at Reliant.

Right: It is apparent from this shot of the Regal 3/25 just how much the Carmel had in common with its three-wheeled relation, with a similar nose and rear styling.

Below: The completed prototype Carmel pictured just off the A5 near Reliant in Tamworth.

Below right: To appease the Israeli market, the Carmel was restyled to omit the reverse slant rear window, which had not been well received.

This is one of a series of photographs taken in March 1962 of a pre-production Carmel, which were sent to Autocars in Israel. *Pat Afford*

With production of the Sussita and the Carmel fully under way, Shubinsky was now interested in exporting cars to the USA. However, he came to realise that the current range of vehicles was not that popular in America, and decided that an open-top sports car would be much more appealing.

Sabra Sport

In 1960, while he was at the Sports & Racing Car Show in London, Shubinsky came across the Ashley 1172 bodyshell, which was designed for an open sports car, produced in fibreglass, and exhibited by a company called Ashley Laminates. With a forward-hinging bonnet and glass-covered headlamps, the bodyshell looked the part and was made to fit either an Austin 7 or Ford 8 chassis. The at the same show he also spotted a new ladder-type running chassis that was fitted with independent front suspension and a Ford Consul engine. Developed and manufactured by Leslie Ballamy, it was intended for a model known as the E B Debonair. Shubinsky felt that it looked about the right size for Ashley's bodyshell. Convinced of his plans, shortly after the show Autocars bought the design rights to both Ashley's 1172 bodyshell and Ballamy's chassis. Subsequently Shubinsky contacted Reliant once again and gave it the task of mating the two by assembling a prototype within fifty days, believing that it would be a pretty straightforward task.

In reality it was anything but, proving quite a challenge for Reliant's engineers. Led by Colin Fine-Thompson (E. S. Thompson's son), with David Page from the Engineering Department and Ken Wood from the Body Development Department, the team faced a number of difficulties in not only mating the new fibreglass bodyshell to the running chassis but also making a number of systems and components fit inside the shell.

Sourcing an engine also had its issues, as the planned engines were too big. However, it was soon discovered that the 1,703cc engine from a Ford Consul fitted under the bonnet and was easily incorporated into the chassis. It was also easily accessed, as the whole front end of the body tilted forward to expose the engine and front suspension. Producing 72bhp, the engine was mated to a German ZF four-speed synchromesh gearbox. Colin Fine-Thompson and his team did the best they could by raiding numerous parts bins of a variety of cars, including the Austin Cambridge and Standard Vanguard. Various three-wheeler components were also used, including coil springs from the Reliant Regal Mk VI and a windscreen from the Meadows Frisky three-wheeler, while the rear lamp units were from the Alfa Romeo Giulietta Sprint. However, in his book *Rebel without Applause*, Daniel Lockton points out that Colin Fine-Thompson recollected that British lamp

Colin Fine-Thompson headed the development team to build the Sabra Sport prototype, Reliant's first sports car.

The Ballamy chassis, Ford engine and ZF gearbox used for the Sabra Sport prototype. *Pat Afford*

15

manufacturer Lucas was so appalled at Reliant's use of 'foreign lamps' that it laid down tooling at its own expense to copy the Alfa units so that Lucas-branded lamps could be incorporated.

Once Reliant had the outer fibreglass shell, its engineers realised that they just did not have the time or budget to complete an inner fibreglass shell. So, just like its older side-valve three-wheeled brethren, the new vehicle incorporated a floor pan made of marine-grade plywood, while the dashboard consisted of nothing more than a flat panel covered in leather cloth and equipped with an assortment of dials and switches. As the new car was destined for the American market, one thing Shubinsky also insisted upon was that the car had large chrome overriders at the front.

When Shubinsky saw the first prototype, which was painted red with a black interior, he was delighted and gave it the model name Sabra Sport. Even though the prototype was not complete – it was missing a wiring harness and propeller shaft – it was exported from Tamworth to the USA where, in May 1961, it made its first appearance at the New York World's Fair at the New York Coliseum.

Reliant had agreed that it would supply Autocars with the Sabra Sport CKD kits for assembly in Israel before shipment of finished cars to the USA. To help oversee and assist the process, Colin Fine-Thompson was sent to Israel, only to find that the parts sent by Reliant to make the bodyshells were impossible to assemble. As a result, while new shells were being developed, Reliant built the first

The Sabra Sport prototype at Reliant with its soft top raised. Note the indicator lamps attached to the top of the bonnet (hood). *Pat Afford*

Above: Another shot of the Sabra Sport prototype with its soft top down. Just visible are its highly decorative wheel embellishers. *Pat Afford*

Right: The 1,703cc Ford Consul engine used in the Sabra Sport prototype. It was mated to a German ZF four-speed gearbox. *Pat Afford*

100 Sabra Sport cars in the UK and shipped them to the USA on Autocars' behalf, whilst the Israelis were still busy preparing their workshops for manufacture of the new design.

The importation (and distribution) of the Sabra Sport into the USA was handled by Sabra Motors Corporation of America in New York (SMCOA). Although billed as a sports car boasting a top speed of 115mph (185km/h), the Sabra Sport initially hit a few snags that prevented it from actually finishing a race, let alone winning one. That state of affairs ended on 27 August 1962, and SMCOA wrote a jubilant letter to Colin Fine-Thompson at Reliant, proclaiming:

'A 61 Sabra won overwhelmingly in a divisional championship race in the F production class. There were 18 cars in that race, including nine Porsches with MGAs, Sunbeam Alpines and one Mercedes-Benz 190 SL representing the balance. This

A Sabra Sport partially assembled before being mounted onto the chassis. The large thick hose (the main heater blower motor hose), with the small heater/coolant hose in the top of it, is hung to keep it out of the way during assembly. *Pat Afford*

This 1968 Autocars brochure for the Sabra Sport notes 'Nothing could be finer than a Sabra'.

An early Sabra Sport with body-coloured bumpers. *Thomas Touw*

was the first time that a Sabra ever finished a race. In every previous race they overheated badly and had to quit in the middle of the race. This time the engine kept normal temperature throughout the race. One of the Porsches is known to be the fastest on the East Coast but came in as a very bad second. It was wonderful to see the valiant Sabra walk away from that Porsche and from the rest of the pack on every corner and widening the gap all the time.'

The car in question was owned by a dentist and had been built in early 1961 as production model No 29. The letter goes on to say that it had

'...the twin SUs in it (not original Alexander), the 4.5:1 rear axle, racing camshaft, light flywheel and only a 8.4:1 compression ratio.'

In 1962 the Sabra Sport was modified slightly with a revised front end and doors, and a Sabra GT (Gran Turismo) was added to the range, fitted with a fixed hard top. The hard top later became an option, with model names introduced denoting ST for Soft Top and HT for Hard Top. Unfortunately the Sabra Sport just did not take off in America as well as it had been hoped. Despite the early surge of orders, interest soon faded, with American sales ending in 1964 with just 144 British-made and 41 Israeli-made cars having been imported.

Autocars plodded on with the model, managing to sell small numbers in Belgium as late as 1968, although all ties with Reliant were severed in 1965 when Shubinsky signed a deal with British Leyland. By 1971 Autocars had entered liquidation.

The Sabra Sport is, to date, the only Reliant-designed sports car to have been featured on a postage stamp. This one was issued in December 2014 in Israel to commemorate Israel's Automotive Industry and to note that the Sabra Sport was the first sports car manufactured in Israel.

Once production of the Sabra Sport was in full swing, a fixed top version was also introduced, which further accentuated the body lines.

Together with the fixed-top Sabra Sport, there was also a detachable hard top for owners with open-topped models. *Thomas Touw*

Sabre (SE1)

After producing the Sabra for the export market, Williams' number two as Deputy Managing Director, Ray Wiggin, had become curious as to whether such a vehicle would be successful if sold in the UK. Seeing an opportunity, Reliant therefore converted two left-hand-drive Sabra Sport cars (chassis Nos 92 and 93) to right-hand drive and changed the spelling of 'Sabra' to 'Sabre' to make the model name more British. Exhibited in 1961 at the Motor Show at Earls Court, London, the Sabre was Reliant's first four-wheeler for the British market and marked the company's entry into the prestigious world of sports cars. Given that the car was originally designed for the American market, its reception was heavily divided; both the public and dealers were unsure of the Sabre's independent front suspension, especially the large boomerang-style chrome overriders that dominated the

front of the car. While the car was very much a Sabra at heart and retained its fibreglass body, a number of key changes were incorporated, such as wire wheels, a fibreglass dashboard, inner door trims and a new steering wheel.

Codenamed SE1 (SE being derived from the first and last letters of the car's name), the Sabre (later known as the Sabre Four) was powered by a 1,703cc Ford Consul 375 engine. In its standard form this provided 72bhp, which was enough to propel the Sabre up to 93.7mph (151km/h) with a 0-60mph (0-96km/h) time of 14.4 seconds, and still provide a fuel consumption of around 27mpg.

With the Sabre came a new badge, which was to set the tradition of Reliant sports cars, including a bladed weapon (whether it be a sabre or a scimitar) as part of its design.

The Sabre made its UK debut at the 1961 London Motor Show, still complete with its controversial large chrome overriders, which led to mixed opinions about the car.

who can resist the *Sabre*

Who indeed?—for the **Sabre's** attraction is not merely superficial—beneath that stylish eye-catching body lies the heart of a top-class sports car.
The "Sabre" is a quality production car designed and built by the makers of Britain's top-selling three-wheeler, whose experience in producing vehicles having inherent qualities of stability, serviceability and lightness combined with strength second to none.
It is available as an open two-seater with folding hood, or in Hardtop or Gran Turismo form.

In an effort to boost the power a little further, the engine was available with either stage 1 or stage 2 tuning modifications, both of which were undertaken by tuners Alexander Engineering Co of Haddenham. The first stage offered a minor boost to the overall performance with a single-choke Zenith downdraft carburettor. The second stage of tuning came with an extra £52 10s added to the price tag and included twin SU carburettors. This gave the Sabre more power, pushing it beyond the 100mph (161km/h) mark on the speedometer.

The first sports car brochure issued by Reliant for the Sabre in 1961 actually used the three-wheeler to promote it, noting that it was 'built by the makers of Britain's top-selling three-wheeler, whose experience in producing vehicles having inherent qualities of stability, serviceability and lightness combined with strength second to none.'

This publicity shot for the Sabre was later edited by Reliant to create a more rounded rear wheel arch, which improved the overall look of the vehicle. *Pat Afford*

While boasting sporty lines, one of the criticisms aimed at the Sabre was the lack of faired-in headlamps, which would have given the front end a much neater appearance. *Pat Afford*

Costing £1,164 19s 9d, the Sabre was more expensive than many of its rivals, and while a number of road testers believed that it offered fairly good handling as its independent front suspension system worked very well, there were some who criticised it, considering the ride to be far too harsh. In response to this, the Reliant engineers worked out that the car handled much better when complemented by Girling combined coil springs and shock absorbers at the rear and a modified live rear axle located by a Watts linkage.

In 1962 the Sabre Six was introduced, with the Sabre Four continuing to be produced alongside. The Sabre Six now featured a short nose together with other slight body modifications that were incorporated progressively into the Sabre Four. The Six was also offered in fixed-head form, classifying it as a 2/4-seater, although the rear space was severely cramped and somewhat impractical. Towards the end of production the last eight Sabre Fours to be manufactured received the short nose that was fitted to the Sabre Six. In total just 208 cars were built, with only 55 of them being sold in the UK; the others were all exported.

who can
resist
the
Sabre

As the cover of this 1961 Reliant brochure suggests,
'Who can resist the Sabre'.

Above: Comedian Ken Dodd is seen here in a Reliant Sabre, but contrary to popular belief he informed the author that he never actually owned one although he said he did enjoy driving it. This one was lent to him for a short period in 1962 by Argyle Motors in Birkenhead.

Right: Shortly before production of the Sabre ceased, the final version included faired-in headlamps, although it still retained its large chrome overriders.
Thomas Touw

The rear view of the Sabre shows the wonderfully sculptured wheel arches and small boot (trunk). *Thomas Touw*

Never wasting an opportunity, and in a bid to raise the profile of the Sabre, Reliant entered the original GT prototype in the Tulip Rally in June 1962, where it was driven by Arthur Rusling and Peter Easton. Unfortunately, while they finished the course, they had to retire due to Easton falling ill during the event, causing them to lose time. This marked Reliant's entry into motorsports and did not deter the company from competing in more events.

Reliant entered the Sabre GT in several more rallies and, while its success was somewhat mediocre, it did manage to come third in its class at the 1963 Monte Carlo Rally. More importantly for Reliant, the rallies not only helped associate the Sabre with the sporting world, but they also tested the cars to the maximum, enabling Reliant to improve upon the components that failed and thus make the cars more competitive.

Deciding to revamp the Sabre and fit a six-cylinder engine, at Ray Wiggin's request Reliant's Eddie Pepall created a number of drawings that, while resembling the original Sabre, now included a much shorter nose and subtle changes to the rear of the body.

Before being phased out, the Sabre Four featured the short nose that was standard on the Sabre Six. *Dave Poole*

While the Sabre had been predominantly an open-top vehicle, the Sabre Six was the opposite, with almost all cars having a fixed top; only two open-top Sixes were manufactured.

Sabre Six (SE2)

Compared with other sports cars of its time, the Sabre was not only beginning to appear quite dated visually, but also mechanically, with other sports cars outperforming it. As a result, in October 1962 a new – more powerful – version of the Sabre (the Sabre Six) was displayed at the London Motor Show, where it was very well received with all three display cars being sold. Reliant's in-house publication, the *Reliant Review*, quoted Sales Director Tom Scott as saying:

> 'Interest in the Sabre Six has amply justified the company's faith in the car. Our entry into the British four-wheeler market after our success with four-wheelers abroad has been proved to be a very worthwhile venture.'

Taking on board the general opinions of the front end, the bodywork had been redesigned to incorporate the shorter-nosed bonnet – thus producing a shorter car by 7 inches (17.8cm) – that was designed by Reliant's Eddie Pepall, together with more rounded rear wheel arches. A number of changes were also made under the bonnet, which saw the inclusion of a more powerful 2,553cc Ford straight six engine, demanding alterations to the chassis. The new engine was now mated to a four-speed synchromesh manual Ford gearbox. For those who wanted more power, an optional three-carburettor conversion and Borg Warner overdrive was also available, together with other options that included a hard-top conversion and either wire wheels or Ace 'Mercury' wheel trims.

With a new Salisbury rear axle, disc brakes fitted at the front and drums at the rear, early versions kept the same suspension, although after just seventeen models had been made this combination proved to be troublesome. To fix it, Reliant switched to a double wishbone and coil system (which was also the standard set-up used on the Triumph TR4) that was supplied direct from its designer and manufacturer, Alford and Alder. With a basic price of £840 (£1,015 11s 3d including purchase tax), the Sabre Six went on sale in 1963. At the 1962 London Motor Show Reliant also exhibited the Sabre Six GT. Costing £890 basic (£1,075 19s 7d with purchase tax), this also used a one-piece moulded fibreglass body fixed to an ultra-rigid box-section steel chassis.

Legendary comedian and actor Norman Wisdom sits in his newly acquired Sabre Six in 1963. The Sabre (and the Scimitar that followed) were always firm favourites among celebrities. *RSSOC*

Far from sparse, the Sabre Six offered the driver an array of instruments. *Dave Poole*

Above: Reliant was always keen that its sales representatives used its vehicles. Here four main area salesmen stand next to company-issued Sabre Sixes. From left to right, they are Jim Lowrie for Scotland, Dermot Slater for the Northern Counties, Hugh Baugh for the South and East, and Bill Woolley for the Eastern Counties.

Left: All Sabres featured a hinged-forward bonnet that offered unparalleled access to the engine, front suspension and ancillaries. *Tony Heath*

In October 1963 a large fire ripped through the fibreglass shop on the south side of the A5, and production of Reliant's three-wheelers (in this case the Regal 3/25 and 5cwt van) came to a complete standstill as all the moulds to make the bodies were destroyed. The Sabre Six, however, miraculously escaped the ravages of the flames as, just a few weeks earlier, the moulds for making the bodies had been moved to a new location. In addition to a new fibreglass shop at Two Gates, Reliant purchased a new factory at Shenstone, which was to be used as Reliant's new engineering factory. It was officially opened on 27 November 1963 by World Champion racing driver Jim Clark.

With a claimed top speed of 120mph (193km/h), the Sabre Six GT proved to be a formidable opponent and, as with its predecessor, Reliant entered it into a number of rallies; in 1963, driven by Roger Clark and G. H. F. 'Bobby' Parkes, it came first and second in its class at the Alpine Rally. Combined with other successes, including finishing third and fourth at the Monte Carlo Rally, by the end of that year Reliant was able to claim that, after its first full year of international rallying, it was the only British manufacturer that season to have suffered no team retirements due to mechanical failures.

In 1964 two Sabre Sixes were entered into the Monte Carlo Rally, and a spectacular crash showed just how strong the Six was, and indeed demonstrated the virtues of a fibreglass body. While driving up a mountain, 'Bobby' Parkes and Arthur Senior (who was driving) suffered a burst tyre just after a hairpin, which caused the car to swerve off the road. At that point of the road there was no retaining wall and the Sabre Six drove over the edge, rolling 80 feet down a scree slope and landing nose-first on the road they had just driven up. Amazingly, both Parkes and Senior climbed out of the wreckage with just a few cuts and bruises, and even hoped to continue driving the car to the finish line. Sadly, despite protecting its crew, the Sabre Six was beyond repair and was towed back to Reliant to be dismantled. Perhaps of greater

Neither the Sabre nor Sabre Six went into rallying half-heartedly and were often pushed to the max. *John Valler*

Still surviving to this day, Sabre Six 42 ENX. *John Valler*

A Reliant Sabre Six taking part in the Monte Carlo Rally in 1963. *John Valler*

testimony to the car was that the only modifications made to the vehicle were extra headlamps, required as a result of using sodium bulbs. The body was a standard one that was fitted to all production cars.

Although privately owned Sabres continued to enter several rallies, for Reliant rallying came to an end. Compared with larger manufacturers, Reliant was at the time only a fairly small engineering company and as such could not afford the level of investment necessary for ongoing rally product development. Furthermore it seemed apparent that its involvement in motorsports was not reflected in increased sales of the Sabre to the public, and the works cars were sold off. That said, the Sabre was to have one final moment of glory when in May 1964 a Sabre Six, driven by Reliant dealer Graham Warner, set a new record at Snetterton Circuit. Driven non-stop for 24 hours, the Sabre Six completed 621 laps, a distance of 1,684.34 miles, at an average of 70.18mph (113km/h).

The Sabre gained some success in the rallying world and Reliant was quick to use wins to its advantage, listing them in its advertising for the Sabre.

The Sabre and Sabre Six were two of only four Reliants to be officially homologated for motorsport with full FIA paperwork (the other two being the Reliant Scimitar GTE and Reliant Kitten).

During the 33rd Monte Carlo Rally in 1964, a Sabre Six overshot a hairpin and dropped 70 feet down a mountainside onto the road it had just driven up. Such was the strength of the chassis that both occupants walked away from the crash with just superficial injuries. *RSSOC*

From this angle it can be seen just how steep the mountainside was that the Sabre Six came down. *RSSOC*

Following Reliant's rallying days a number of Sabres still compete in historic rallying and racing, using the cars as they were intended. *Thomas Touw*

Despite gaining those successes in rallies, and indeed celebrity endorsements from owners like film star and comedian Norman Wisdom and hit parade singer Danny Williams, the Sabre Six was not a great seller. With only seventy-five Sabre GTs and two Sabre convertibles being made, the Sabre range came to an end in 1964. Remaining stock was sold alongside its replacement; the Scimitar GT.

Left: Not put off by the 1964 incident, Reliant was back with a Sabre Six, 660 XYB, for the 1965 Monte Carlo Rally. *Dave Poole*

Below: More than 50 years later, Sabre Six 660 XYB can still be found on the track, as seen here at Curborough Sprint Course in 2017. *Dave Poole*

The hard-top version of the Sabre, which incorporated a dummy roof vent.

Sabre SE3

It was always felt that the Sabre was underpowered, so Reliant began to build a V8-powered model codenamed SE3, fitted with a Ford V8 engine. However, the project was soon abandoned in favour of the SE4.

Rise of the Scimitar

Scimitar GT (SE4)

Sales of the Sabre were a lot lower than anticipated and Reliant's co-founder, Tom Williams, remained uncertain about manufacturing sports cars, believing that Reliant was doing perfectly well with its three-wheelers. Ray Wiggin, however, was keen to prove that sports cars could be just as profitable, although he was also aware that in-house designs for the Sabre's replacement were probably going to fare no better.

Believing therefore that Reliant needed to engage an external stylist, and one that could meet Reliant's modest means, Wiggin visited the 1962 Motor Show at Earls Court in London for inspiration, and it wasn't long before he found it.

The Daimler SP250, the chassis of which was used as a base of the Ogle SX250. *Giles Chapman Library*

A car on the Ogle stand at the show soon caught his eye. Conceived by David Ogle (of David Ogle Ltd, later known as Ogle Design Ltd) the car, an Ogle SX250, was built on the Daimler Dart SP250 chassis, in which was installed Daimler's 2.5-litre V8. Wiggin deduced that the SX250 body was about the same size as the Sabre and potentially would fit on the Sabre chassis. Reliant approached Ogle Design and asked to buy the rights for the SX250, although they were not for sale. In its wisdom, however, Reliant saw the potential in Ogle and engaged with the company to work on other designs, including the FW4 (Rebel), an economical four-wheeled passenger vehicle.

The Ogle SX250 had been commissioned by Boris Forter, Managing Director of the Helena Rubenstein (UK) company. However, in May 1962, halfway through its development, David Ogle was killed in a car crash while driving another Ogle creation, the Ogle Mini SX1000. John Ogier (Ogle's business partner) then became Chairman while former Ford designer Tom Karen became both Managing Director and Chief Designer. Karen completed the SX250 design together with the interior, getting the prototype car ready for the Motor Show. Six SX250s were planned and a second was built for Forter after he gave the prototype to his mistress. Fortunately for Reliant, the planned buyers for the remaining four vehicles did not materialise as intended.

Above: Boris Forter, Managing Director of Helena Rubenstein (UK), with one of the Ogle SX250s that he commissioned in 1962. *Giles Chapman Library*

Right: The Scimitar GT is instantly recognisable from this front shot of an Ogle SX250. *Giles Chapman Library*

It has been claimed that the SX250 was then destined for production by Daimler, and although Daimler's owner, Sir William Lyons of Jaguar, is said to have liked the design, Tom Karen confirmed in an interview with the Reliant Motor Club that the SX250 design was never offered to Jaguar as a replacement for the Daimler SP250.

With no buyers, the SX250 design had now become redundant, although Wiggin did not give up and continued to show interest. Following further dialogue between Ogle Design and Reliant, a deal was sealed and Reliant finally acquired the design.

Further examination of the SX250 showed that it was actually only 2 inches (5.1cm) longer than the Sabre. Furthermore, while sharing an identical front track, the rear track of the Sabre was just 1½ inches (3.8cm) wider. It seemed therefore that Wiggin was correct, and that the body would indeed fit the Sabre chassis with minimal modification. Development commenced on the new vehicle (codenamed SE4) with the modified body being modelled at Ogle. The clay model then became the basis for the master from which Reliant made the patterns for the moulds that would produce the production bodies. David Page of Reliant's engineering department set about modifying a Sabre Six chassis with an elongated wheelbase, while Ken Wood of body development worked on the bodyshell.

Reliant's body construction method differed substantially from David Ogle's; the latter used shells supported by square tubes, whereas Reliant specified inner and outer shells like a metal body with metal tubes inside them. Taking a master from the Ogle mould, Wood remodelled it to create a completely new body. While it was important that the design remained as a sports car, it also need to be a 2+2 Grand Touring car. Don Pither, in his book

The Scimitar GT, seen here with Ray Wiggin, made its first public appearance at the 1964 Earls Court Motor Show in London. An economy four-wheeler, the Reliant Rebel, as depicted in the poster in the background, was also making its first appearance.

The Scimitar and its Forebears, notes that Ken Wood stated that the rear seat 'was a joke' as it offered no leg room whatsoever. As a result this had to be moved back 6 inches (15.2cm), meaning that the whole roof line also had to be extended backwards to provide headroom. This then meant that the front doors had to be lengthened by 5 inches (12.7cm) to provide entry to the rear seats. Other more subtle changes were also made, including rounded wheel arches and minor changes to the style of the front end. While modifications were made to the chassis to incorporate softer Aeron Rubber assist-springs, under the bonnet the new GT retained the same straight six Ford engine from the Sabre Six. This was now equipped with triple SU carburettors as standard, which increased the power to 120bhp and provided a top speed of 117mph (188km/h). Choosing a name that connected the new

model with the Sabre and showed that they both came from the same stable (or perhaps the same forge), Reliant chose the name Scimitar. Interestingly, at the same time it also registered the name 'Swordsman', although that name was never used.

The Scimitar GT (or Scimitar Coupé as it is also known – although, as Tom Karen points out, it was intended as more of an executive saloon than a coupé) made its first public appearance at the 1964 Earls Court Motor Show in London, where it sat alongside Reliant's other new four-wheeler, the Rebel, which was aimed at the economy car market. With a price tag of £1,292 1s 3d, including purchase tax, the Scimitar drew much admiration from both the public and the press, making the Reliant stand a hive of activity throughout the duration of the show. The press was full of praise for its sleek design and performance figures, with 0-60mph (0-96km/h) in just 10 seconds, a

With chassis number 003, and displayed by Reliant at the 1964 Earls Court Motor Show, this particular vehicle is classed as the first true Scimitar GT to be built. Chassis 001 was never used on a finished car, while chassis 002 was registered as an Ogle Scimitar. *Matt Greenly*

Above: Having mastered its skills with its three-wheeler range, Reliant was second to none when it came to handling fibreglass. Here the rear section of a Scimitar GT is being moulded ready to be removed, then hand-finished.

Opposite: The Scimitar GT assembly line. Some cars are covered in aprons to protect the polychromatic paintwork finish as various parts are fitted.

Left: Reliant's first Scimitar brochure came in the form of this tri-coloured publication of 1964.

figure that was on par with that of the Lotus Cortina, one of its main competitors. Coupled with wire spoke wheels and comprehensive instrumentation as standard, a number of optional extras were also available that included a radio, front seat belts, electric sun roof, a ZF-type gearbox, and a choice of the de Normanville model 230 overdrive unit. The Scimitar GT stood out as a desirable and very competitive executive saloon.

The chassis and all major pressings for the 120 m.p.h. Reliant Scimitar GT are produced by PRESS OPERATIONS LTD.

Left: In addition to the Scimitar GT chassis, a number of other major pressings were made in-house under Reliant's subsidiary company, Press Operations Ltd. Pictured is a 200-ton press that performed 225,000 separate pressings each week.

Above: Press Operations Ltd had its own publicity material that notably details its involvement with the Scimitar GT. *Pat Afford*

While the car was lavished with much praise, road testers soon discovered that the new Scimitar GT suffered as a result of using the same rear suspension as the Sabre. Edward Eves, Midlands editor of *Autocar*, raised such concerns with Ray Wiggin and advised him on what he considered would be one of the most economical ways to address it. This was to turn the top leading arms upside down on either side of the vehicle and also include a small Watts linkage that would allow a sideways location for the axle. This worked well and significantly improved handling.

The wire spoke wheels fitted to the Sabre and early Scimitar GTs did much to enhance the sporting appearance of the vehicle. *Martin North*

When first unveiled, the Scimitar GT won much praise for its elegant lines and style.

The Scimitar GT was known as a 2+2 although the seating capacity was defined as three adults (with occasional fourth seat) or two adults and two children. *Martin North*

In 1965 the body design of the Scimitar GT was further lauded when Reliant made its very first entry into the Institute of British Carriage & Automobile Manufacturers' Coachwork Competition. The Scimitar GT was entered in class 11 for cars with an enclosed coachwork costing between £1,000 and £1,200 exclusive of purchase tax. It then made history by winning a silver medal and becoming the first car with a fibreglass body to win an award.

Above: The Sabre featured a sabre blade within the design of its badge, and the theme was carried across to the Scimitar GT, although now showing a single scimitar. *Dave Poole*

Right: Like many other sports cars of the era, the Scimitar GT used separate Lucas lamp units at the rear for stop/tail, indicator and reverse illuminations. *Harvey Payne*

The Ogle GTS (Glazing Test Special) commissioned by Triplex Safety Glass with its 66 0GLE registration plate. *Thomas Touw*

The sheer amount of glass used in the Ogle GTS is evident in this photo. *Thomas Touw*

Triplex Ogle GTS

In 1964 work began on a one-off Scimitar in the form of the Triplex Ogle GTS (Glazing Test Special). Triplex Safety Glass Co Ltd, makers of automotive safety glass, commissioned Ogle Design to design and build a show car that would demonstrate new glass technology in the form of laminated Sundym glass and advanced techniques including direct glazing. Rather than start with a completely new body from the ground up, Ogle decided to adapt the Scimitar GT by redesigning the body upward from its waist. While Triplex designed the car's glazing to provide minimum pillar widths, Ogle developed a full estate-type rear end that gave a maximum compartment for four people while also incorporating a structural roll-bar to offer protection to the occupants.

Together with a wire-heated front windscreen and backlight (these used crimped wires with each wire being one two-thousandths of an inch in diameter), the GTS was covered in 43 square feet of safety glass with a heat-absorbing glass roof and curved-round side glasses. The Sundym glass used in both the roof and side glasses contained a trace element of ferrous oxide. This helped to increase the absorption of ultraviolet and infrared rays, which reduced the transmitted radiant heat into the car's interior (this itself having a matt finish to help reduce glare). Abandoning traditional glazing techniques, the glass in the car was bonded directly to the body, negating the normal rubber sections.

Featuring the distinctive number plate 660 GLE (illegally re-spaced as 66 0GLE), the Triplex Ogle GTS was featured at the 1965 Motor Show at Earls Court, London, on the Ogle stand. Following the show it was driven to the Turin Motor Show by two automotive journalists (Basil Cardew of the *Daily Express* and Tom Wisdom of the *Daily Mirror*), where it was admired by many leading Italian designers and voted as the showpiece of the exhibition.

When the car returned to the UK, the GTS also became the first Reliant to be used by the Royal Family. It caught the eye of HRH Prince Philip, who bought the vehicle in 1966 and caused a media furore when he arrived in it at London Airport. The Prince was travelling to Oslo for the British Trade Fair and used the car to travel from Buckingham Palace to the airport. The *Daily Express* wrote at the time that millionaire Nubar Gulbenkian, the Earl of Snowdon and Princess Margaret were also interested in it. The Prince used it for his own personal use for around 18 months, and the car was then repurchased by Triplex and loaned to the National Motor Museum at Beaulieu. In 1969 it also appeared at the Grand Prix at Silverstone, where the Clerk of the Course used the GTS as his official car. Years later, it was purchased by Reliant enthusiast and author Don Pither, and on his death in 2002 was shipped to the USA, where it is now owned by former Ogle designer Professor Carl Olson.

afterwards at various shows in Geneva, Frankfurt and Amsterdam, where it soon found a place in the European market. Furthermore, interest in the new Scimitar was such that Reliant's Sales Director, Tom Scott, was now negotiating with companies in the USA and Canada that were also interested in importing the car. With a slightly higher top speed of 121mph (195km/h), the new improved version, while still having its critics, was found to handle much better and sales were starting to pick up and look very encouraging indeed.

Right: Ray Wiggin enjoys a road test report of the 3-litre Scimitar GT in the *Sporting Motorist* dated November 1966.

Below: In this striking pose of a 1966 Scimitar GT, worth noting is the position of the number plate. Reliant stated that it was styled into the car at a position that could help direct fresh air into the engine compartment to assist cooling. *Thomas Touw*

The Scimitar GT is seen here in 1967 with a sliding roof that was offered as an optional extra. Behind the car is another Reliant product, the Scooter Ski, which was manufactured by Reliant for Scooter Ski Ltd in Nottingham.

The Scimitar was further improved with the introduction of a Scimitar GT SE4b specification in late 1966. The main changes were a revised interior that now featured a new centre console and switch layout; these kept the car up-to-date and maintained sales volumes.

In 1967 an oil embargo began on 6 June on the second day of the six-day Arab-Israeli war, which limited oil shipments to the UK and other Western countries. With petrol supplies threatened, the concept of a 3-litre car suddenly seemed most inappropriate to many, so Reliant combated this by also offering a more economical 2.5-litre version, which was also around £120 cheaper. Using a V6

Even though during its production run the Scimitar GT lost its wire spoke wheels, the cheaper steel wheels with chrome embellishers that replaced them still combined well with the overall shape of the body.

Ford Essex engine that provided a top speed of 111mph (179km/h), this became the Scimitar GT SE4c. The Scimitar GT continued in production until November 1970, although from 1968 it was sold alongside its successor, the Scimitar GTE.

Scimitar GT Automatic

In 1966 Reliant also started the development of an automatic transmission version of the Scimitar GT, which, as Sporting Reliant enthusiast Dave Poole points out, 'was more of a development car rather than a prototype.' Scimitar GT chassis number 66 was converted to an automatic transmission format and, it is believed, was one of only two Scimitar GTs to be built to that specification. An automatic option was never made available for standard production and sale. One of the development cars is still known to exist; it was owned by Reliant until around 1970, when it was sold to a private owner.

While the Scimitar GT was never available with automatic transmission, this particular example was a development vehicle with an automatic gearbox. *Dave Poole*

The developmental automatic gearbox as fitted to chassis number 66. *Dave Poole*

FW6 (Rebel GT)

In its standard form, Reliant's Rebel economy car was somewhat limited when it came to speed; the Rebel 1600GT would have certainly changed that, although it did not reach production.

When the Scimitar GT was initially exhibited in 1964 at the Earls Court Motor Show in London, Reliant also introduced a new four-wheeled economy car called the Rebel. While its history is not within the scope of this book, following its introduction one of the biggest criticisms about it was the lack of power as a result of its 598cc engine, which was carried across from the three-wheeler range. Reliant soon reasoned therefore that a more powerful engine was required and began to experiment with a Rebel 1600 GT prototype (codenamed FW6). With minimal changes to the chassis, the GT version was fitted

with the 1,599cc Ford Crossflow engine that was used in the Ford Cortina (Mk 2) 1600E. Once road legal, the prototype was thoroughly tested and it was soon discovered that it outperformed its sportier brother, the Scimitar GT. Reliant had inadvertently created the forerunner to the 'hot hatch' long before such vehicles caught on. With the Scimitar GT being the company's sportster, the FW6 was not put it into production and Reliant decided instead to increase the capacity of the 598cc to 701cc, giving the standard Rebel model more torque.

The reign of the Scimitar GTE

Scimitar GTE (SE5)

While the Scimitar GT was a success for Reliant, the interior was not exceptionally spacious, and although it had four seats it was only really classified as 2+2 and essentially only suitable for two adults with two children in the back. Ray Wiggin felt that better seating room in the back would give the Scimitar more appeal, so explored whether the Scimitar GT could be extended into a true four-seater with plenty of luggage space.

A close view of the Scimitar GTE prototype grille that covered the headlamps. *Tom Karen*

This mock-up of an extended Scimitar GT was rejected by Ray Wiggin in favour of the Scimitar GTE. *Tom Karen*

A side view of the mock-up of the Scimitar GTE at Ogle Design, which was immediately approved by Ray Wiggin as soon as he saw it. *Tom Karen*

Tom Karen, at Ogle Design Ltd, was approached and came up with a number of ideas. One of these included extending the rear of the Scimitar GT Coupé bodyshell. Karen notes that

> 'Using a coupé shell as a base we started modelling two options, one on each side. On the right-hand side the greenhouse was extended leaving a short "duck back". This work was done by a talented Australian designer [Bryon Fitzpatrick] while I was taking a brief holiday.
>
> On my return a number of ideas that I had been playing with my mind came together and I had a clear vision of the estate-type body I wanted to propose.'

Karen firmly believed that, rather than expanding the Scimitar GT into a larger version, it was much better to create a new model from scratch, while retaining as many of the original features as possible. In September 1967 Ogle set about creating a clay model of what was to become the GTE (Gran Turismo Estate, or, as it later became known by Reliant employees, Great Tamworth Express).

The clay model featured a raising waistline and a dropping roof line at the rear to give the car a much sportier appearance. During its development, while Ray Wiggin was at the 1967 London Motor Show, Tom Karen asked him to call in at Ogle on his way home to view the model. The shape was something totally radical for its time and Karen admits that he felt somewhat nervous as to how Wiggin would view it. He recalls:

> 'We mocked up this version in preparation for a visit by Ray Wiggin. I was very confident about the estate-type body but

feared that it might not click with Reliant's conservative view of design. To my great relief Ray backed it without hesitation. A brave decision because the car that became the GTE design was so very controversial. He gave the go-ahead for the prototype body to be built.'

Having rejected the extended Scimitar GT version and deciding there and then that the new GTE was the shape Reliant would be going for, within ten days of Wiggin seeing the mock-up and briefing the Reliant board, approval was given for it to go ahead. Ogle Design then created a GTE prototype at its studios at Letchworth that cleverly used the doors, windscreen and bumper from the Scimitar GT. While the rear of the car fell easily into place, styling the front was

In February 1968 the prototype leaves Ogle Design's HQ at Letchworth heading for Reliant in Tamworth. *Tom Karen*

The man behind the design of the Scimitar GTE, Tom Karen of Ogle Design Ltd.

The Scimitar GTE prototype was completed in January 1968. *Tom Karen*

somewhat more troublesome. It proved very difficult to develop the design of the front end to match the revolutionary design at the rear.

The prototype featured four round headlamps, two on either side of the front end, fixed behind rectangular open grilles. When the prototype was completed in January 1968, it was driven from Ogle at Letchworth to Reliant in Tamworth for evaluation.

As the GTE was longer than the Scimitar GT, Reliant's Chief Engineer, John Crosthwaite, decided to scrap the original notion of increasing the GT chassis by 7 inches (17.78cm) and set about engineering a completely new running chassis. The new concept included outriggers and perpendicular rails, which offered greater side impact protection. A new wider Salisbury axle was used together with stiffer springs, and the engine was positioned further back in the chassis to help balance the weight distribution on the axles.

Well before hatchback vehicles were the norm, the GTE fibreglass body also incorporated a feature that, with the exception of earlier vehicles like the Austin A40 Countryman and Renault 16, was pretty much unique for its time. The rear was accessed via a glass tailgate, hinged at the top. In early vehicles this was supported by a spring arm, although this was later replaced by gas struts. Tom Karen also notes that

'Apart from pioneering the sporting estate formula, the waistline of the GTE went up all the way to the back. Many people found this hard to swallow, but this feature has found its way on to every car designed since then (with notable exceptions – Rolls Royce and top-end Mercedes cars). The long roof on the GTE had significant aerodynamic benefits: lower drag, lower lift and great cross winds stability... The roof had a little "kick-up" at the end, which worked sculpturally and aerodynamically. The glass rear hatch was flat (a cost saving) and extended downwards to give good vision when reversing.'

Inside, the GTE had a similar dashboard to that fitted in the Scimitar GT but, more importantly, it had four large armchairs, two in the front and two in the back, each separated by an armrest. The rear seats were also radical for the time as they folded down, providing ample luggage space in the rear; in addition, the rear armrest hinged forward when the seats were folded flat, stopping luggage from sliding forward into the cockpit area. This provided a luggage capacity ranging from 19 to 36 cubic feet depending on the seat configuration. Generally delighted with the prototype, Wiggin requested a few changes that included a restyled front nose and grille, modified rear ventilation and 14-inch wheels, before finally making the decision that the GTE was ready to go into full-scale production.

Pre-production Scimitar GTE RRE 162G on test in Tamworth immediately after being built.

When superimposing the Scimitar GTE outline over that of the Scimitar GT, the longer wheelbase and increased headroom and luggage space at the rear are immediately apparent. *RSSOC*

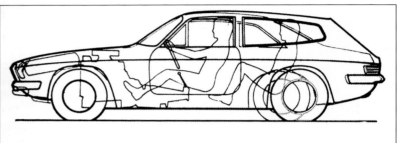

The rear styling of the Scimitar GT (left) compared with that of the Scimitar GTE. *Martin North*

A cutaway Scimitar GTE during the car's launch at the 1968 Motor Show.

In October 1968 the new Scimitar GTE (SE5) appeared at the Motor Show in London and the world's first ever sporting estate car was born. Initially, feedback was quite mixed, with some people loving the concept while others did not like it at all. Tom Karen recalls that:

'The bit that was hard to swallow, even by some Ogle colleagues and the motoring press, was the rising waistline – the line between the body and the greenhouse that went upwards all the way to the back. This had never been done before and offended many traditionalists, but is now part of virtually every model on the road.'

Whatever the views, once journalists took the Scimitar GTE out on road tests most were very impressed with its capabilities. It captured a niche in the market, being the only production car at the time that offered high cruising speeds, could seat four adults in comfort, and had good luggage space as well. Furthermore it looked like nothing else on the road at that time and so clearly stood out from other cars. Powered by a 2,994cc

JOIN THE GTE SET!
—with the new Scimitar GTE

Grand touring elegance *plus* estate versatility

Reliant's first Scimitar GTE brochure invited you to 'Join the GTE set', proclaiming that only the GTE offered the benefits of a grand tourer and a capacious estate in one car.

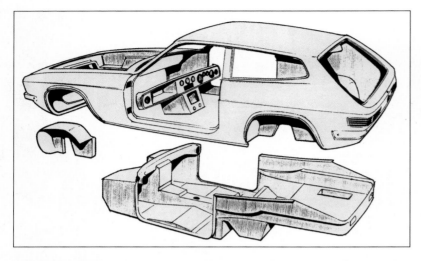

The Scimitar GTE consisted of two main bodyshells, outer and inner, the latter forming the floor pan. Two smaller sections were then used around the front wheels to form an inner wheel arch.

Unlike other motor manufacturers, Reliant bodies continued to be completely handmade. Here a mould of the upper shell of a Scimitar GTE is prepared before being hand-layered with fibreglass matting.

Designed by John Crosthwaite, the Scimitar GTE chassis had the engine positioned so that the weight was concentrated amidships and kept well down.

Like the upper shell, the floor pan was also handmade by building up layers of fibreglass matting, although this was built over a mould rather than in one.

Ford Essex engine producing 136bhp, the Scimitar had a top speed approaching 120mph (193km/h) and delivered between 22 and 28mpg. It was priced at £1,759 including purchase tax (plus an additional £64 for an overdrive unit). Reliant was willing to sell and paint a GTE 'any colour on earth – or the moon' and did receive an order from one lady requesting that it be painted the same colour as her nail polish. In general, though, most purchasers tended to stick to the standard range of colours: Golden Sands, Satin Silver, Mexican Red, Manhattan Blue, Everest White and Caribbean Green.

Also on display at the same motor show was a unique version of the Scimitar GTE created by Ogle Design Ltd and built for Sir Julian Hodge's wife Moira (Hodge at that time being Reliant's chairman

For a short while both the Scimitar GT and GTE were made side-by-side, until the former was phased out in 1970.

and effective 'owner'). Differentiating from the Reliant version, the Ogle Scimitar featured, among other things, electric retractable headlamp covers and a glazed roof section. The interior was furnished in light tan with leather and chequered fabric seats, which were complemented by bronzed window glass. At the rear of the vehicle the chrome name letters were stuck on the rear glass hatch, which was something new at that time.

Ogle Design Ltd said:

'The new and exciting 3-litre Scimitar by Ogle, based on the Reliant GTE, incorporates a number of extra features which give this new concept car an even more futuristic look. Apart from the large windscreen and glass roof over the front seats, the most striking difference is the frontal grille area. The Ogle Scimitar has a concealed headlamp system which embodies four of the new Lucas "all-glass" rectangular sealed beam units, with electrically operated shutters. These 60/60 watt light units are a result of two years development work, and offer all the advantages already associated with the sealed beam principle. When the headlamp shutters are closed, the light units are fully protected and the full frontal area of the car has a flowing and distinctive appearance.'

In addition, Tom Karen noted that

'The headlamp covers, later removed, were meant to be "fail safe" by folding down if there was a malfunction.'

Following the show the Ogle Scimitar GTE was passed over to Moira Hodge and was owned by the Hodge family until 2014, when it was sold on, reappearing for sale in 2017 and again in 2018.

The 1968 Motor Show was a great success for Reliant, and so many orders for the GTE were placed that it created a three-month waiting list. The GTE was also backed up by a network of almost fifty dealers throughout the UK, guaranteeing a 24-hour turn-round for spare parts. Reliant claimed that this after-sales service rivalled that of any car sold in Britain.

Scimitar GTE
Scimitar GT coupé

TEST DRIVE TWO WINNERS FROM RELIANT NOW!

Both the Scimitar GT and GTE found success in the export market. Here both models are loaded on board, bound for Australia. *Dave Poole*

The Ogle Scimitar GTE shortly after its completion with electrically operated shutters over the headlamps and a glass roof over the front seats. *Tom Karen*

From this angle the Ogle Scimitar GTE's glass roof over the front seats is clearly visible. *Dave Poole*

The spacious interior of the Ogle Scimitar GTE was finished in light tan with leather and chequered fabric seats. *Dave Poole*

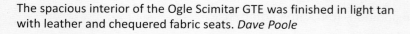

Above: Later in its life the Ogle Scimitar GTE had its headlamp covers removed, which gave the vehicle quite a different look. *Thomas Touw*

Right: Here is one of Reliant's first press images depicting the Scimitar GTE (SE5), which also showcases the spoked fibreglass wheel trims that were used on early models and gave an alloy wheel appearance.

One thing that owners noticed about the Scimitar GTE was how dirty the rear window became, so for the 1969 British Motor Show Reliant introduced another motoring first and fitted a rear wiper and washer so that the window could be cleaned. When designers at Ogle believed that a rear wiper would be something fitted to all performance cars in the future, they were not wrong. The GTE also had a petrol filler cap at the rear of the vehicle

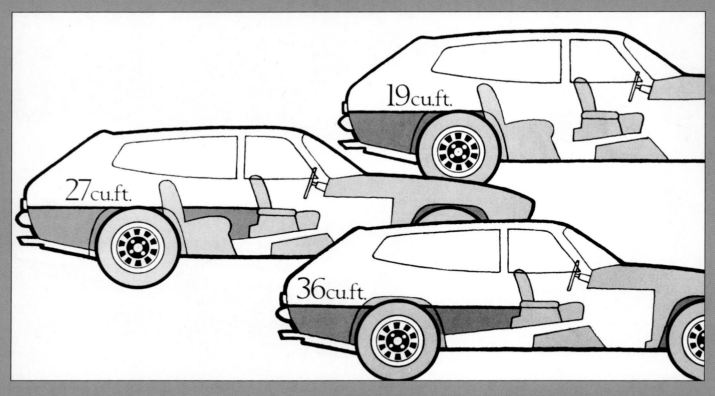

With various seat configurations the Scimitar GTE offered 19 cubic feet of luggage space as standard, 27 cubic feet with one rear seat folded down, and 36 cubic feet with both rear seats folded down.

Scimitar offers the impossible

Up front: bred like a racehorse. 0-60 in 8.6 seconds.
Takes the motorway at a cantering 70 with 50-plus in reserve.
At the back: space for a cartload – anything from golf bags to Glyndebourne hampers. 19 cubic feet with all four seats up; 27 cubic feet with one back seat down; 36 cubic feet with them both down.
In between: comfort for four adults. The taut, road-hugging ride that only a thoroughbred Grand Tourer will give.
And surprising economy – you can get up to 28 m.p.g. or even more with careful driving.
An impossible combination? Test drive it. That's all we ask.

To: Marketing Services, Reliant Motor Company Ltd., Tamworth, Staffs, B77 1HN.
☐ Please send me more details about the Scimitar GTE.
☐ Please arrange a road test.   ☐ If under 18 tick here.

Name
Address

Present Car
2205032

Scimitar GTE
HIGH PERFORMANCE ESTATE

between the tail lamps; this also caused a few complaints from owners as the pipe behind the cap to the fuel tank was right-angled and made filling awkward. Reliant therefore modified this so that the connection to the fuel tank was straight, which instantly aided refuelling. Due to the number of enquiries, Reliant also introduced an optional three-speed automatic Borg Warner 35 gearbox. The 1969 Motor Show was a superb success for Reliant, netting more than £1 million in orders. The price of the GTE now stood at £1,875 15s 3d for a manual model and £1,998 3s 2d for the automatic.

Such were the GTE's looks that in 1970 it won a beauty pageant. Following an invitation by the Guild of Motoring Writers to a dinner that was hosted by TV personality Richard Baker, a contest was held to find the 'most beautiful body'. Baker called in various ladies

This particular advertisement for the Scimitar GTE in 1968 presented a superb analogy. The GTE was in essence a racehorse offering 0-60mph (0-96km/h) in 8.6 seconds (very respectable for the era) while the back offered a cartload of space.

This particular 1969 Scimitar GTE is the first Reliant sports car the author can recall seeing while at boarding school in 1977. The car was (and still is) owned by one of his former school teachers, Bob Cole.

clad in swimsuits who were playing the roles of Miss Coventry, Miss Luton, Miss Dagenham and Miss Longbridge. Then to a triumphant fanfare Miss Tamworth was announced, and a Scimitar GTE bodyshell was carried onto the ballroom floor and crowned 'Britain's Most Beautiful Body'.

In October 1970 Reliant announced that from 1971 the interior of the GTE would be available in two colours. Until then all interiors had been black, but additional options of Tan and Willow Green were also to be made available, together with a new range of external colours comprising Nevada Yellow, Acacia Green, Mexican Red, Satin Silver, Everest White and Caribbean Green, or the option of any other colour at an additional cost of £39 3s 4d. By popular demand more options were available that included cast alloy wheels, Pirelli Cinturato HR high-speed tyres and a Radiomobile stereo tape-player/radio.

The Scimitar GTE received a tremendous boost in 1970 when HRH Princess Anne was spotted driving a new Satin Silver example in London. The car had been loaned to her by the Kenning Motor Group on trial, and it must have made quite an impression as, shortly afterwards, Reliant received an order for a new GTE from Buckingham Palace. Reliant was under Royal command not to reveal Princess Anne's new car order until it had been handed over.

Finished in Aircraft Blue with grey leather and a Radiomobile stereo tape-player/radio, the Palace insisted that the Royal GTE be a normal production car and not a special one-off version. The car was then presented to Princess Anne as a combined 20th birthday/Christmas present from the Queen and other members of the Royal Family. It was registered 1420 H, which reflected Princess Anne's position as Colonel-in-Chief of the Royal 14/20th Hussars.

Ray Wiggin looks rather pleased at this line-up of Scimitar GTEs in the compound in 1970. Also notable are other Reliant products in the background, with the four-wheeled Rebel and three-wheeled TW9, Regal 3/30 saloon and the Supervan.

Take off for the 'seventies-

- in a Scimitar GTE

When the news became public, former Reliant employee Brian Grice was working for the *Tamworth Herald* newspaper. Upon informing the *Herald*'s Deputy Editor, Dave Moore, about the Royal order, Moore asked him, 'Are you sure about this?' Once the story had made the *Tamworth Herald* the mainstream press was quick to follow up on it, with numerous newspapers highlighting the Princess and her new mode of transport.

Perhaps the most poignant report, which shows just how the GTE was viewed at that time, comes from Christopher Wilkins of the *Birmingham Post*:

'You can hardly fault Princess Anne on her taste in motor cars. Her choice of a Reliant Scimitar GTE not only makes excellent sense by any motoring standards, but also shows her to be a thoroughly fashionable young woman.'

With the onset of the 1970s, Reliant used an aeronautical theme proclaiming that the Scimitar GTE was a new car for a new decade and that no other vehicle was better able to meet the speed and space demands of the 1970s.

An iconic shot of the Scimitar GTE with the Royal Air Force Red Arrows swooping low over it. The photo was promoted by the *Sunday Express* as one of the most striking advertising photographs in 1970.

Princess Anne formed a great bond with the Scimitar (and indeed other Reliant vehicles, such as the four-wheeled Kitten and the three-wheeled Robin), and went on to own eight Scimitar GTEs that also included a Middlebridge Scimitar GTE, which HRH still owns at the time of writing.

Production of the GTE was in full swing when in January 1971 the production line hit its first hurdle. Workers at the Ford Motor Company's Dagenham, Halewood and Swansea plants walked out after rejecting a £2 wage increase. As a result Reliant was no longer being supplied with the Ford V6 engine. Using existing stock, production was able to continue as normal until the sixth week of the Ford strike. After that Reliant had to resort to building

Right: Another Reliant first came in the form of a rear screen wiper, which was fitted to the Scimitar GTE from 1970, then consequently copied by virtually every other car maker.

*Bottom right:*The automatic Scimitar arrived in 1970, when Reliant offered a Borg Warner 35 automatic gearbox as an optional extra on the GTE.

Below: With the Scimitar GTE, Reliant had built an absolutely unique vehicle and was keen for it to be seen as a luxurious car that would be at home both on a farm and at a country estate.

The Scimitar GTE received a Royal boost in 1970 when Princess Anne was seen leaving Buckingham Palace with one on loan, having been made available by Reliant through the Kenning Motor Group. *RSSOC*

One of numerous varieties of Reliant Scimitar GTE posters that decorated the walls of Reliant dealers up and down the country throughout the 1970s.

The Scimitar GTE's lifting rear hatch allowed superb access to the rear luggage space and was something that subsequently appeared in numerous models offered by other manufacturers. *Dave Poole*

the GTE just three days a week with no engines. This had a huge impact and it wasn't until May 1971 that Reliant was able to start building GTEs at the rate of thirty cars a week once more. By that time around 250 vehicles had been lost as a result of the strike.

It was in the same year that Reliant introduced its 'common sense price policy'. This set out to eliminate the abundance of optional extras that the motoring industry tended to add on to vehicles to minimise the impact of the basic purchase price.

Forget the 120mph, remember the 34.1mpg.

The rear of this 1970 postcard hastens to remind the reader that despite the sporting prowess of the Scimitar GTE, it is also a surprisingly economical car (for its era and type). *Good Motoring* magazine of April 1975 reporting 34.1mpg on a 200-mile journey.

Of particular note on this 1971 Scimitar GTE are the GT alloy wheels that were fitted to the loan car that Princess Anne used in 1970. The wheels have subsequently become known as 'Princess Anne' wheels and in recent years have become highly sought after.

A mock-up of the Rogue 700 (FW7), which was designed as a mid-engined sports car and destined to use Reliant's economy engine from the three-wheeler range. *Peter Stevens*

FW7 (Rogue 700)

In 1969 Reliant explored designing a small mid-engine sports car, although as it used a Reliant engine and the drive train from its economy range the vehicle carried the codename FW7 rather than a SE moniker. That said, close examination of photographs of the FW7 reveal that it carried the name 'Rogue 700' (700 denoting the 700cc engine) and the proposed front badge included dual scimitars similar to those used on the Scimitar range, suggesting that the vehicle may have slotted into the sports car range.

Reliant built a full-sized mock-up of the car in 1970, but it was soon realised that the 700cc engine would not be powerful enough to give the vehicle any kind of performance, so the project was terminated. Two years later Fiat brought out a very similar concept in the form of the diminutive Fiat X/19.

The proposed badge for the Rogue 700, with its dual blades, clearly shows a sporting link with the Sabre and Scimitar. *Graham Hodgson*

From the side it is apparent just how similar the Rogue 700 was to the Fiat X/19, even though it predated the X19 by two years. *Tom Karen*

An alternative design by Ogle Design for the FW7 mid-engined sports car. *Peter Stevens*

Upon acquiring Bond Cars in 1969, Reliant inherited the tooling and manufacturing rights for the Bond Equipe Mk II, which, like the Scimitar, used a body made of fibreglass.

FW8 (Bond Equipe)

Another potential sports car for Reliant, which again carried an 'FW' codename, was the FW8. In 1969 Bond Cars Ltd, another manufacturer of three-wheelers, was up for sale and, like Reliant, it also produced a sports car called the Bond Equipe, which had been introduced in 1963. Designed by founder Lawrie Bond, the Equipe was built on a Triumph Herald chassis and was powered by the Triumph Spitfire's 1,147cc engine. In 1964 Bond introduced a more powerful version with a 1,296cc engine, and this was uprated once more to a 2-litre Triumph Vitesse engine in 1967 with the introduction of the more refined Equipe 2. Due to its close association with Triumph, the Bond Equipe was sold through Triumph dealers, and this was something that greatly interested Reliant. Following an agreement between Ray Wiggin and British Leyland Motor Corporation Ltd's Managing Director George Turnbull that if Reliant purchased Bond, the Scimitar could join the Equipe in having access to Triumph dealers, Reliant purchased Bond Cars Ltd in February 1969. However, shortly after the acquisition BLMC's chairman Lord Donald Stokes pulled the plug on the handshake agreement.

However, all was not lost; the Bond Equipe still looked a very lucrative business, as it maintained access to Triumph dealers up and down the country. In addition, as the Equipe mainly used Triumph parts, there were no expensive redesigns to consider. Also the Equipe's fibreglass body presented no issues at all to the pioneering Reliant, as it was one of Europe's leaders in the composite process. Reliant started to upgrade the Equipe (then codenamed FW8) and initially continued to use Triumph components, with the intention that it would ideally be eventually re-engineered to use Reliant's own. As Donald Pither details in his book, *The Scimitar and its Forebears*, there was every chance that Reliant saw the Bond Equipe as a 'Junior Scimitar', and as such it would have been priced below the Scimitar GTE. As head of the body development team, Ken Wood eliminated the use of mixed Bond and Triumph panels and produced a revised one-piece fibreglass bodyshell, from which he created a mock-up of the FW8. However, by this time Reliant was leasing Bond's plant in Preston, Lancashire, and soon realised that it was not suitable for full volume production of the FW8. With the Tamworth site already working at full capacity on

Initially Reliant planned to continue the Bond Equipe and started on a new project (codenamed FW8) to produce a mock-up for a replacement.

While retaining key styling elements of the original Bond Equipe, Reliant's design was far more rigid than Bond's in that it used a one-piece bodyshell.

Artwork concept for the FW8 based on a redesigned Bond Equipe. *Martin North*

Book your free test drive now!

As a special Motor Show offer, we are able to arrange free road tests, any-where in Britain, of two very popular Reliant Motor Group vehicles. Just indicate the car of your choice on one of the coupons below and post to:

Mr Rodney Hackett,
Reliant Motor Company Limited,
Tamworth, Staffordshire

Reliant Scimitar GTE

The only 120 miles an hour, 4-seater grand tourer estate; available in manual or automatic versions.

Please arrange a free road test for me of the Scimitar GTE.

NAME
ADDRESS
TELEPHONE NUMBER

Bond Equipe 2 Litre

An elegant sports four-seater, offered as a saloon or a lively convertible.

Please arrange a free road test for me of the Bond Equipe 2 Litre.

NAME
ADDRESS
TELEPHONE NUMBER

For a short while in 1969 it was possible to test drive both the Scimitar GTE and the Bond Equipe at Reliant.

several profitable models, both three- and four-wheelers, there was just no room for the FW8 there and the project was quietly dropped. However, the Bond name was to re-emerge as one of Reliant's three-wheeled vehicles, the Bond Bug, in 1970.

Further enhanced in 1972, the Scimitar GTE (now codenamed SE5a) incorporated a number of improvements while outwardly maintaining its originality.

Scimitar GTE (SE5a)

Despite the success of the Scimitar GTE, Reliant did not rest on its laurels and continued to introduce improvements. After an overhaul, an improved version was released in October 1972. This was named SE5a and launched as a 'Smoother Scimitar'. Reliant announced that the changes were an ongoing continuation of the common-sense price policy and an attempt to include more features as standard. As such the prices were increased by £132.83 on both the Scimitar GTE and Scimitar GTE Overdrive models, making them £2,379.39 and £2,463.73 respectively inclusive of taxes.

The interior of the SE5a was updated with a new vacuum-formed ABS plastic fascia using a laminated sheet, newly developed by ICI, which provided a soft-feel skin of leather look-alike material. Fitted with new rocker switches (instead of the older-style toggle switches) and new warning lights for a number of functions, the interior also saw a host of other changes that included footwell vents to improve ventilation and seat belts,

With the Scimitar SE5 having used the same Scimitar badge as the SE4, it was given a slight redesign for the SE5a. *Dave Poole*

The Scimitar GTE (SE5a) brought with it a new rear lamp cluster that included a reversing lamp. The cluster unit was jointly developed with Lucas by Reliant and Lotus, although Jensen also went on to use it. *Martin North*

which were now fitted as standard. The trim continued to be offered in either black or tan together with a new option of leather seat facings.

Another feature of the SE5a was a new vacuum-formed ABS plastic fascia, fitted with new rocker switches and warning lights.

In July 1975 Princess Anne visited Reliant to tour both Tamworth sites (Two Gates and Kettlebrook) and the engineering site at Shenstone. The Princess drove herself there in her third Scimitar GTE.

The Scimitar GTE was just as successful for the export market; this particular example currently resides in Switzerland. *Roger Gut*

Externally the GTE offered four new exterior colours (Highland Purple, Shetland Blue, Wessex Green and Mediterranean Green) and a slightly higher nose cone, which raised the height of the front lamps by 2 inches (5.1cm) so that they complied with new vehicle regulations. Together with a new grille, new Scimitar shield logo badges were added to the side of the front wings and new door handles specified. The chrome strip along the side was removed and a new set of lamps introduced at the rear that now included reversing lights in the cluster. Reliant's Supplies Manager at that time, Barrie Wills recalls that:

> 'The new rear lamp cluster on the SE5a presented Reliant with a rare opportunity which allowed Tom Karen at Ogle more design freedom than usual. Concurrently, Colin Chapman was developing his first four-seater Lotus, the second generation Elite. Such was the strength of the relationship between the two totally different specialist car company heads that Ray Wiggin and Chapman decided to share the investment in brand new tooling with Joseph Lucas Electrical so that, for the first time, Reliant could avoid specifying a proprietary Lucas lamp while the Norfolk company avoided "borrowing" one from a volume car producer's "parts bin". The tooling cost was shared pro rata to each company's somewhat modest anticipated sales volumes. A few months later, the chief buyer of Jensen approached me for permission to use the same lamp cluster on their new Jensen-Healey. Lotus' purchasing director, Richard Morley, agreed with me that we should allow it on the basis of the same volume-based cost formula. Jensen's over-inflated volume expectations for their ill-fated sports car resulted in a welcome and over-generous bonus rebate to both Reliant and Lotus.'

The engine was also slightly improved, with a new inlet manifold being introduced, which, together with a new carburettor, increased the power from 138 to 145bhp. This gave the car a top speed of 125mph (201km/h).

In 1972 sales of the Scimitar GTE had increased by 58% compared with the previous year and were showing no signs of slowing down. The car received more modifications for 1974 in order to produce a more executive-type Scimitar; among other things, these included rear seat belts and quartz halogen headlights. Three addition external colours were also added – April Yellow, Florida Green and Venetian Blue – together with the former range of five colours. Unfortunately, Scimitar GTE production was hit again by industrial action from 1 January to 7 March 1974 as a result of a coal-miners' strike, although Reliant was able to resume full production again from 8 March. Towards the end of the year, as a result of the economic climate, demand for the Scimitar GTE had reduced considerably, with the long waiting list for the vehicle being dramatically shortened. As a consequence, in conjunction with Hodge Finance Reliant offered a special 9.5% interest finance scheme for all versions of the Scimitar GTE and the three-wheeled Robin van, which ran from December 1974 until January 1975. This compared with the average 16.5% interest schemes that were in place with other cars in the UK. Things looked very different just eight months later when registrations of the Scimitar GTE grew by 9.7% in a year, with August 1975 seeing an all-time record of 248 new registrations.

One 4x4 vehicle was built with the revised running gear and chassis and for many years it remained at the back of the Reliant development department slowly decaying away. Having failed to promote the idea by seeking approval from the Reliant board to turn it into an official development project, John Crosthwaite eventually convinced Ray Wiggin to sell him the car, and it was restored by Crosthwaite and registered for the road. Years later this unique 4x4 Scimitar GTE was sold to a private collector and resurfaced in March 2018 when it was sold at auction.

Scimitar GTE (SE6)

Ray Wiggin was all too aware of criticisms thrown at the GTE for having a cramped interior space, and it was following another order from Princess Anne that he decided to provide a GTE for her that was both more comfortable and had more leg room behind the front seats. As a result, in 1974 he initiated a development programme led by Ken Wood, head of Reliant's body engineering team, to look into increasing the leg room. To determine what dimensions would be suitable, Wood and his team cut an SE5 bodyshell in half, in line with the rear door opening, and set about inserting 4 inches (10.16cm) extra into the wheelbase and making the doors 2½ inches (6.3cm) longer. This became the basis of Princess Anne's new car.

Scimitar GTE (SE5a 4x4)

Reliant sports car enthusiast Dave Poole holds within his Sporting Reliants archive data showing that in 1973 a one-off Scimitar was built that used four-wheel drive technology by Tony Rolt (from FF – Ferguson Formula) as adopted by Jensen for its FF model, based on the Interceptor. With the assistance of Ted Laban (Senior Sports Car Designer) and Os Webb from Ferguson, Chief Engineer John Crosthwaite initiated an unofficial project by redesigning the Scimitar GTE chassis, enabling it to incorporate front-wheel drive. The engine and gearbox mountings were also revised to support the increased weight of the GKN differential and to achieve drive past the Ford 3-litre engine and clutch housing to the front differential and to also maintain steering geometry. The steering rack was also moved to clear the GKN front differential unit. A torque split of 40/60 was specified and the drive to the front differential was taken from the rear of a special overdrive gearbox by Hi-Vo chain and propeller shaft containing two constant velocity joints.

Based on an original Scimitar GTE chassis, the 4x4 chassis was developed by Reliant in 1973, although it remained a one-off. *Dave Poole*

A mould for the larger Scimitar GTE (SE6) was created by literally cutting an SE5 bodyshell in half both down the middle and across the body. A 4-inch (10.16cm) section of fibreglass was then added to increase the size.

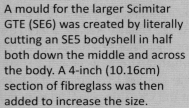

A test was carried out at MIRA in 1975 to determine whether the larger SE6 body had much impact on seat movement during a collision.

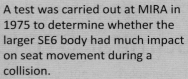

Then, to help increase comfort, especially for people on the larger side, the decision was taken to cut another body in half down the middle and increase the width by 3 inches (7.6cm) to further enhance the extra length of the Royal GTE.

On hand was Tom Karen of Ogle Design, who was engaged to restyle the new Scimitar GTE to give it a fresh look while at the same time keeping the distinctive look of the SE5 series. While Karen was somewhat unhappy about the wheelbase extension, which he felt impacted negatively on the overall aesthetics of the vehicle, the end result was a larger, much sleeker-looking vehicle that provided increased interior space with both extra leg room and

Right: The 1975 brochure for the larger Scimitar GTE (SE6) notes that with the new version, with the rear seats folded down, the total luggage space had increased from 36 to 40 cubic feet.

NEW SCIMITAR GTE

A BIGGER ALL-ROUND MOTORING EXPERIENCE

Above: Even with four adults on board, the Scimitar GTE still offered a bigger than average load area.

Left: With plush, thick carpets, deeply cushioned velour-covered seats (or leather as an optional extra) and a comprehensive dashboard, the interior of the Scimitar GTE was totally luxurious.

elbow space. This, Ray Wiggin believed, would attract the growing market for executive sporting cars. Dubbed the SE6, the new Scimitar GTE was instantly recognisable by its larger twin headlights and black moulded polyurethane bumpers. Other exterior changes had also taken place with the removal of the quarter-light windows and the replacement of the expensive chrome-plated brass finishes by more affordable Jaguar-style chrome iron sections, a move that Reliant stated gave the GTE a 'corrosion-proof' exterior. The exterior colours were also changed again, with Alaska Blue, Celtic Brown and Cygnet Grey being added to the range, while Highland Purple was dropped. This meant that the customer had a choice of ten standard exterior colours.

A cutaway Scimitar GTE was featured at the launch of the enlarged SE6 model at the 1975 Motor Show. *Barrie Wills*

The interior was also completely redesigned and now featured a new black fascia moulding that incorporated an abundance of proprietary Smiths instruments, including a cluster shared with Triumph. The seats were also more luxurious and more substantial, with the rear seat now consisting of a bench seat cushion with individual folding backrests. In addition, the doors, now 4 inches (10.16cm) wider, meant that access to the rear seat was much easier. Trimmed in nylon with leather cloth sides and backs, the seats helped the SE6 to appeal to the executive market. To help raise the standard further, increased soundproofing was fitted together with numerous features that were now being added as standard. These included electric windows, electric aerial, internally adjusted door mirrors, headrests and rear seat belts. An abundance of optional extras was also offered, including leather trim, power steering, and a Phillips RN 642 stereo radio and cassette player.

Following the design of the SE5 chassis, a new chassis was developed for the SE6 that had extended box sections. While fitted with the same suspension units, it was necessary to incorporate a wider axle and a wider steering rack. As an additional bonus, extra room within the engine compartment allowed for the optional fitting of power-assisted steering. A larger petrol tank now held 20 gallons of fuel, three more than the SE5 series.

Below left: The restyled nose of the Scimitar GTE (SE6) featured a deeper, flatter grille with a Scimitar nameplate above it

Below: Two-tone paintwork was a popular choice with the Scimitar GTE (SE6). Note also the Wolfrace alloy wheels, which became an optional extra in 1977.

Reliant advertising aimed the Scimitar GTE (SE6) towards the executive, and this photo was taken at the world-famous Belfry golf course near Sutton Coldfield. Note also the rubber bumper mouldings that now adorned the car.

The SE6 made its debut at the Earls Court Motor Show of 1975 and its success was such that Reliant pulled in £3 million worth of orders from the show and numerous applications for new dealers. Using the same engine as the SE5, the SE6 came in two versions, the overdrive version for £4,367.61 and the automatic for £4,446.00 (both prices including car tax and VAT). It was made available to the public in January 1977.

Scimitar GTE (SE6a)

Shortly after the SE6 was launched it became apparent that the new design had created unforeseen problems with the front suspension settings. The front springs and dampers were too soft, causing customers to complain of bottoming and sluggish handling. Reliant responded by fitting uprated Girling units, and changed units on existing vehicles under warranty. Even though the SE6 was a more civilised machine than its predecessor and much better for long-distance touring, a number of other niggles were also being reported. Customers' complaints included the power steering being too light, body flexing, and doors dropping on their hinges. After just 1,550 SE6 models had been built, by late 1976 Reliant had addressed all these issues with the SE6a.

Although the SE6a was virtually identical visually, with no external changes made, the chassis was now much stiffer and suspension settings were modified to improve handling. In a bid to make the Scimitar GTE an even better car, and even though there had been no complaints concerning the brakes, the braking system was improved, specifying Lockheed 10-inch brake drums on the rear instead of Girling 9-inch drums, and Lockheed disc brakes at the front.

Reliant anticipated that 1977 would be the most significant year yet for the Scimitar GTE, with a new export programme being launched for the SE6a, so it increased production from thirty-five vehicles a week to fifty with the introduction of a night shift.

Jaguar's Chairman, F. R. W. (Lofty) England, had retired to live in Austria, so Ray Wiggin and former Jaguar apprentice Barrie Wills, by then Reliant's Deputy Managing Director, persuaded him to use his European contacts to establish a European export network. This was a very successful programme and by August of that year the Scimitar was being sold in Austria, Switzerland, Belgium, Holland, Greece and the Faroe Islands. Constantly striving to ensure a good choice of colours, another four were added to the range with Russet Red, Dolphin Grey, Greengage Yellow and Quartz Green. These replaced Alaska Blue, Beaujolais Red and Cygnet Grey.

A Scimitar GTE (SE6a) bodyshell, outnumbered by its three-wheeled brethren, being flatted down ready to re-enter the paint shop. *Thomas Touw*

Above: A Scimitar GTE chassis being built up with running gear and various components at Reliant in 1978. *Thomas Touw*

Above right: Looking at the same line from the opposite end, a Scimitar GTE body waits to be mounted to its chassis and running gear. *Thomas Touw*

Right: With body and chassis combined, work can begin on the interior, as seen in this 1978 shot. *Thomas Touw*

Below right: Further along the production line more components are added, such as the lamps and bumpers. *Thomas Touw*

Below: Once the chassis is completed the body is carefully lowered into place and the vehicle starts to move along the production line. *Thomas Touw*

In this 1978 shot most of the exterior components have been fitted, minus the glass, and work has begun to fit the dashboard, door panels and interior trim. *Thomas Touw*

The front end is clearly visible here; the frontal area above the bumper is actually solid, despite the dummy grille that is later attached to it. *Thomas Touw*

Towards the end of the build, the glass is added all around the car. *Thomas Touw*

A pair of Scimitar GTEs leave the production line in 1978. *Thomas Touw*

Fitted with 1420 H show plates, this particular Scimitar GTE is believed to be one of Princess Anne's former Scimitars. *Dave Poole*

Reliant's expansion plans
and the Saab Sonett

By the early-to-mid-1970s the Reliant Motor Company had reached what history would later determine to be the pinnacle of its success. Its turnover was constantly averaging more that £20 million a year and the Scimitar GTE was hitting record sales. At the same time production of three-wheelers was running at record highs with around 330 cars being built each week. Added to these were superb export sales of all Reliant vehicles, especially CKD sets to Turkey, which were bringing money in by the bucket load from all around the world. With so much going on it was hardly surprising that

Reliant was the UK's second most profitable motor manufacturer in 1971 and 1972 and, at that time, Tamworth's largest employer, with more than 1,800 employees.

With expansion appearing to be the only way forward, in 1972 Reliant embarked on a £1,750,000 three-year expansion scheme. It planned to increase its factory space by 2½ times from 97,000 square feet to 242,000 square feet, and in addition create an extra 700 jobs, increasing the number of employees to 2,500. While stage 1 of the project created, among other things, a completely new

Like earlier Scimitars, the SE6 enjoyed healthy exports all over the world. This particular vehicle was pictured near Swan River in Perth, Western Australia.
Neil Corfe

assembly hall for the upcoming Robin three-wheeler and a new paint shop with sufficient capacity to paint the body shells of its entire range of cars, stage 2 proposed a second hall for assembling the Scimitar GTE. In addition to the GTE it was planned that a new Saab Sonett would share the same hall, so stage 2 of the project was to be partially financed by income from the Saab project.

Manufactured by Saab Automobile AB of Sweden, the Saab Sonett was a lightweight two-seater sports car built between 1955 and 1957, which, following a short hiatus, had recommenced production in 1966. The car was redesigned in 1970 and was fitted with a Ford 1,500cc V4 engine, although in the USA emission control requirements reduced the performance of the engine drastically, so much so that in 1971 the Sonett was upgraded with a 1,700cc V4

engine, reduced by emission controls to the power output of the 1,500cc model at 65bhp. After 1972 US safety regulations also insisted that new low-speed-impact-proof bumpers be added to cars, which on the Sonett looked completely out of place and changed the characteristics of the original design.

Saab USA's President, Jonas Kjellberg, was interested in creating a new generation of Saab Sonett for the US market and contacted Reliant in 1973 aiming to create a deal in which Reliant would design, engineer and assemble the car. For Reliant such a deal would have pushed ahead the work for the new Scimitar GTE assembly hall in which the GTE and the Sonett could be built in shifts, side by side. Reliant contacted Tom Karen at Ogle Design Ltd, who provided concept drawings of a new Sonett, while Reliant drew up a business plan. Unfortunately, around

the same time sales of the existing Sonett had slumped following the 1973 oil crisis, and Saab announced that production was to end in 1974. Kjellberg presented Reliant's business plan for the new Sonett to the board of Saab Automobiles in Sweden, who rejected the proposals, bringing the whole project to an end. As a result it was one of the deciding factors in Reliant not going ahead with stage 2 of its expansion programme, thus deferring plans for a new Scimitar GTE assembly hall.

Expansion plans for 1972 were initially to create two assembly halls, one for the three-wheeled Robin and another for the Scimitar GTE (seen here in orange). The latter was never built.

Initially the Saab Sonett was destined to be built alongside the Scimitar GTE at Tamworth, although the Saab project was later abandoned. *Peter Stevens*

Like the Scimitar GTE, the Saab Sonett would have been a hatchback-type vehicle with two doors. *Peter Stevens*

Wiggin's passion for a Reliant-built sports car was identified very early on. On 26 May 1961 Colin Fine-Thompson, who had been heading the development of the Sabra Sports car for Israel, sent a private letter to Tom Williams detailing that:

'I think that possibly I alone am more than aware of the cost in human effort that was required to bring the Sabra Sports car up to the production stage in the limited time that it was built in. I am confident that due only to the enthusiasm of Mr Wiggin and his staff, not only was the car completed in record time but has proved to be a highly successful.'

As a result of his enthusiasm and dedication to the company, in 1962 Wiggin became the Deputy Managing Director, then the Managing Director in 1964 shortly before Williams' death. It was also Wiggin who introduced Tom Karen to Reliant and as a result made one of the most important, and probably the bravest, of decisions to go ahead with the Scimitar GTE project.

Speaking of Wiggin, Tom Karen says:

'Ray made all the difference to Reliant when it was in danger of being mired making Regals [the three-wheeler range from 1953 to 1973]. He had a good nose for design and approving the GTE was a bold step not many would have taken. He got a great team together to support him, they showed much loyalty and made huge efforts to achieve results fast.'

Ray Wiggin's daughter, Ruth Kitchen; remembers that:

'Reliant days seem very far away but I still have clear memories of my father's time there. So far as I can remember, he was a very hands-on MD who would do things like collect a car at random from the production line on a Friday evening and drive it home. Then he would spend time driving it "hard" whilst talking into his Dictaphone giving his report on any noises he heard or on the ride quality. Often Ann [Ruth's sister] and I would be in the back of the car enjoying the ride! On Monday morning his report would go in to the engineers and some action would be taken... He wanted to drive the car just as any Reliant customers did and wanted to make improvements if he could.'

Ruth also recalls that:

'In later years he formed his own company and quite a few ex-Reliant employees came to join him so it was like old times in some ways. I worked for him myself until my son was born in 1997. He was a very good employer, fair and of the highest integrity. I am his daughter but I think others would agree with me!'

In 1998 Barrie Wills presented the creators of the Scimitar GTE with framed images to mark the 30th anniversary of the car's market launch. From left to right are Ray Wiggin, Wills and Tom Karen. *Barrie Wills*

Reliant's former Deputy Managing Director, Barrie Wills, who worked alongside Wiggin through most of the 1970s, also agrees and recalls:

'The exact opposite of his auto industry friend and contemporary, Lotus' Colin Chapman, the self-effacing Ray never sought personal publicity or accolades, preferring those to go to his beloved Reliant. The unwelcome Nash takeover of 1977 brought a tragic ending for the man who took Reliant from a turnover of £600,000 to £20 million over less than 20 years. That he was so successful with his international trading company Sherbrook over the 20 years that followed was typical of a hardworking, talented and very focussed businessman.'

Ray Wiggin passed away in December 2011.

Scimitar GTE (SE6b)

Following the J. F. Nash takeover in summer 1977, production of the GTE was cut back and all future development was halted. A problem then arose a few years later in 1980 when Ford discontinued the 3-litre V6 Ford Essex engine and replaced it with the German-built 2.8-litre Cologne engine. In order to continue production, Reliant had little choice but to modify the SE6a to accommodate the new engine, thus creating the SE6b.

Reliant discovered that, although the new engine had similar power to the old model, it had a lower torque, which meant reduced performance. To help recover some of this, Reliant had to reduce the ratio in the rear axle. In addition, due to the size of the engine a number of modifications were also required under the bonnet, which included a redesigned cooling system and an electronic ignition system. Taking advantage of the overhaul, the SE6b also had a mild makeover externally with the nose cleaned up and stripped of lettering and chrome strips. Both were replaced by a single shield-shaped badge. To help increase the model's appeal and retain an executive feel, each model came with electric mirrors, intermittent wipers, halogen headlamps, rear fog lights, a seatbelt warning light, rubber door strips and the introduction of an optional two-tone paint

The Scimitar GTE (SE6b) was most noticeable by its nose, which now omitted the Scimitar name bar and used a deeper black plastic dummy grille.

The SE6b version of the Scimitar GTE was the last that would be produced by Reliant.

scheme. An electric sunroof was also made available as an optional extra. The interior was also improved with a choice of several new upholstery colours, while still retaining the Scimitar's impressive luggage space, which, with the introduction of the SE6, increased from 20 to 40 cubic feet with the rear seats folded down.

The longevity of the SE6b was further increased in 1981 with the introduction of a galvanised chassis, a process that was then specified for all vehicles, both the sports car range and the economy cars. This gave the Scimitar GTE a potentially greater lifespan than almost any other production car in the world.

Stepping back a year, by 1980 the recession that had hit Britain in the late 1970s was biting hard and sales of the Scimitar GTE had decreased dramatically, with just two to three cars being built per week in 1981. This continued until 1985, when it was announced that production of the Scimitar GTE was planned to cease. Production continued until November 1986 with Reliant building Scimitars to order before the last GTE left the production line. This was sent to Princess Anne, making it her seventh and final Reliant-manufactured Scimitar GTE.

Scimitar GTE five-door (SE7)

Not long after Barrie Wills became Reliant's Director of Product Development and Supplies in 1975, he came up with the idea of a five-door Scimitar GTE, inspired by an equivalent Aston Martin of the era. Both he and Ray Wiggin contacted Ogle's Tom Karen to present a few ideas for a five-door version of the Scimitar SE6a that would have a full tailgate between the rear lamps and above the rear bumper. Ogle duly obliged, although both Wiggin and Wills found the renderings and mock-up most disappointing. Wills notes that he felt:

'...the rear side glass kick-up was just too dramatic to the point of being a very poor pastiche of the traditional more subtle GTE interpretation. Also the roof was too flat and, above all, the whole rear quarter was just far too bulky. Ray just didn't like it at all!'

In theory the new model would have been codenamed SE7, although Wills does not believe the SE7 designation was actually applied to the designs, as the idea was so short-lived. Instead, with the help of 'Lofty' England Reliant looked into designer alternatives in Italy.

Scimitar FW11/SE7

Two years later, in 1977, Ray Wiggin was asked by Otosan's Chairman Rahmi Koç to propose a replacement for the Anadol, which had been selling very well in Turkey but was nearing the end of its life. Having been disappointed by Ogle, Reliant developed a vehicle package based upon the interior dimensions of the Fiat 128, the same package that Giorgetto Giugiaro had selected for the first VW Golf, and approached Marcello Gandini at Gruppo Bertone, who came up with a five-door vehicle codenamed FW11. It was planned that the FW11 would replace the Anadol, and four prototypes were built, two being sent to Turkey. Barrie Wills reveals that he thought it too presumptuous to place an Anadol or Otosan badge on the full-size model, so instead chose a Scimitar badge and (even though it was going to Turkey for review by Rahmi Koç) asked Gandini to apply that as the Scimitar brand was planned for the UK version as a Triumph Dolomite Sprint replacement.

The car was a modern style of five-door hatchback that had a number of luxuries including electric windows, which were not usually associated with European cars at that time. Otosan's parent

The proposed five-door Scimitar GTE design by Ogle in 1977 was felt by Reliant to be a poor imitation of the original. *Tom Karen*

Another of Ogle's designs for a replacement Scimitar GTE in 1977. *Tom Karen*

Designed by Bertone, initially as a replacement for the Anadol, the FW11 was then considered to replace the Scimitar GTE. *Onur Selçuk*

Reliant's decision not to use the FW11 design soon became Citroën's gain, when that company acquired it and mass-produced it as the Citroën BX for 12 years.

company, Koç Group, had also been approached by Ford to take over manufacture of the to-be-discontinued Ford Taunus from its Cologne plant, and following Wiggin's departure Koç decided not to adopt the FW11 concept and followed the Ford route instead. Reliant therefore looked into the possibility of replacing the Scimitar GTE with a modified version of the FW11 and restyled the design further, fitting alloy wheels and a Ford 1,600cc engine. The new prototype was exhibited as the Scimitar SE7 at the 1980 Birmingham Motor Show. Although there were plans for a range of vehicles modelled around the FW11 with engines from 1,300 to 2,800cc, the design was taken no further by Reliant, although it was later refined by Bertone for use by Citroën as the Citroën BX.

Scimitar GTC (SE8/SE8b)

The idea for an open-top Scimitar was first initiated in 1977 by Barrie Wills. Prior to the J. F. Nash takeover later that year, Wills created a development plan of future models to present to the board, and among these was a redevelopment of a Marcelo Gandini-designed replacement for the GTE into a GTC version. Wills' GTC would have been a Stag-like derivative of the Triumph, which had just ceased production. It was planned that in conjunction with British Leyland it would have been powered by a Rover V8 3,500cc engine. The idea was approved by Ray Wiggin although following the Nash takeover the plan was scrapped. Following Wiggin's departure and with Ritchie Spencer now at the helm it was instead decided to create a GTC by redeveloping the existing GTE model. Reliant contacted Tom Karen at Ogle Design and asked him to style an open-topped version of the well-established Scimitar GTE, keeping as many panels and fittings as possible from the existing model. With a number of similarities to the Stag, the new Scimitar had a roll-over hoop for safety reasons and a boot at the rear, together with several other minor changes around the rear lights and vent grilles.

Reliant's Ken Wood and his team from the body development department then set about designing the GTC to ensure that the body had sufficient torsional rigidity to prevent the vehicle sagging in the middle. It was soon discovered that the original chassis design already provided all the strength required. Due to the complexity of creating a hood, Reliant decided not to manufacture it itself and outsourced it to Coventry Hood & Sidescreen, making great efforts to ensure that the designed hood matched Ogle's styling. The hood was made from highest-quality German Happich material, replacing the cheaper vinyl that tended to be used in most open-topped cars of that time. Internally, the new Scimitar kept its normal seating layout, although now, when the rear seats were folded down, they provided extra access to the newly designed boot.

The prototype Scimitar GTC based on an SE6a body with a redesigned rear end that incorporated a boot/trunk.

A partial interior shot of the prototype Scimitar GTC, which also shows the roll bar over the front seats. *Martin North*

The prototype Scimitar GTC wearing a 'GTE' number plate. *Martin North*

The first prototype, codenamed SE8, was finished in 1978 and powered by a 3-litre Ford V6 engine. After further development the engine was switched for a Ford 2.8-litre, and in March 1980 the Scimitar GTC was officially launched. Codenamed SE8b (rather than SE8a, possibly to bring it in line with the SE6b) and priced at £11,360, the GTC was, with the exception of the Mercedes SLC (costing around £8,000 more), in a league of its own.

The GTC came with power steering, electric windows, an electric aerial and Wolfrace wheels that, while being on the options list, were pretty much fitted to most vehicles. One of the optional extras for the GTC was a fibreglass hard top, which arrived in 1981 complete with a rear screen heater. Unfortunately the release of the GTC coincided with an impending recession that was hitting the British economy hard, and as a result it did not sell well. Dealers were encouraged by Reliant to offer the GTC at discounted prices, and even Prince Edward acquired one for a short term, although neither initiatives had a positive impact on sales. By 1982 just twenty Scimitar GTCs were being built per year before production came to an end in November 1986, together with the Scimitar GTE. It is said one of the main issues with both models was that following the Nash takeover in 1977 the Scimitar lacked further development. As a result it did not keep up with its competitors and started to look very dated indeed. Ritchie Spencer recalls that

Reliant's range of vehicles, including the Scimitar GTC, are seen here at the 1981 Motor Show.

Unlike the prototype, the production Scimitar GTC used an SE6b body and nose.

Even with its hood up, the Scimitar GTC retained its sporty looks and still offered superb all-round visibility.

Unlike the Scimitar GTE series, which used chrome letters, the GTC was the first Scimitar to use a vinyl transfer for its name badge. *Martin North*

This Reliant publicity shot of the Scimitar GTC actually shows the prototype model with the registration number XJW 247T.

The SE82 was a significant project to develop a Scimitar GTE replacement powered by a Rover V8 engine. *Carl Langridge*

Styled by Bertone, the SE82 project cost Reliant more than £100,000. *Dave Poole*

'Sales of the GTE were going down and down and, while it was not public knowledge at the time, Reliant was in severe trouble. We tried injecting life into it with the Scimitar GTC but it was not enough to make it viable. The decision therefore to cease manufacturing the GTE and GTC was absolutely a financial one.'

Project SE82

Project SE82 was a possible replacement for the existing Scimitar GTE, the '82' signifying the year that Reliant planned to put the car into production. In 1978, after the departure of Wiggin and Wills, Reliant contacted the Italian car stylist Bertone to design a new car as a spacious 2+2 sports hatch with a large glass area. The front styling for the new car was approved in January 1979 when Ed Osmond, by then Reliant's Engineering Director, travelled to Turin to view a clay model. When interviewed by the Reliant Motor Club and asked whether the SE82 project needed to take on board certain design elements of the Scimitar GTE, Marcello Gandini of Bertone replied:

"No it was a fresh design, but keeping in mind that it needed to take in a V8, and that the design could be simply altered to a sports estate too. What we proposed were two slightly different designs in one asymmetrical prototype."

With an overall length slightly greater than that of the Scimitar GTE (SE6) and a planned all-independent chassis fitted with double wishbone suspension at the front and sub-frame-mounted trailing arms at the back, a full-sized mock-up of SE82 was built, together with a complete interior, but the project was soon abandoned.

It was planned that the SE82 would retail at around £15,000 and would be powered by a Rover 3.5-litre V8 engine, but rising petrol costs and increased competition from the sales market meant that

The mock-up of the SE82 interior included an abundance of switches and instruments. *Dave Poole*

discounts offered by larger concerns made it impossible to sell the car at a competitive price, so Reliant was unlikely to sell the car for a profit. This also made it much harder for Reliant dealers. As a result, the company took the decision to halt all further development in March 1980, despite having spent more than £100,000 on the project.

Ford RS200

While technically it was not a Reliant, another sports car was built by the company in 1985 when the Ford Motor Company contacted it to not only produce the bodyshell for the RS200 rally car but also to assemble it as well. With a top speed of 150mph (241km/h), the Ford RS200 was a turbocharged, mid-engined two-seater sports car that employed a number of advanced design concepts including two- or four-wheel drive that was selectable by the driver. It was powered by a 1.8-litre turbocharged 16-valve, double-overhead-camshaft, fuel-injected, four-cylinder engine that developed more than 230bhp and could push the car from 0 to 60mph (0 to 96km/h) in under 5 seconds. The body of the car was designed by Filippo Sapino of Ghia in Turin in conjunction with Ford's design groups.

To comply with rally homologation rules to ensure that a new car could enter the world championships, just 200 of the turbocharged RS200s were built at Reliant's Shenstone plant. The cars were then sold at a retail price of £36,000 each, with priority given to drivers who planned to use them for rallying. While Reliant produced the fibreglass body, Ford provided the chassis and all mechanical components for the vehicles to be assembled, and supervised production of the vehicles.

The assembly line for the Ford RS200 at Reliant's Shenstone plant. While Reliant produced the fibreglass bodies, assembly of the vehicles was supervised by Ford. *RSSOC*

A Ford RS200 at the security gate of Reliant's former engineering premises in Shenstone. *Dave Poole*

This was a potential Scimitar GTE design produced for *Autocar* magazine in 1986 when it asked Ogle Design what it thought the Scimitar GTE would look like if it was still in production. *Tom Karen*

Autocar GTE

Shortly before the Scimitar GTE came to an end, in February 1986 *Autocar* magazine contacted Tom Karen and invited him to show how he believed the GTE should have been developed further had all such work had not been halted in 1977 following the Nash takeover. Karen responded with an updated design that showed a much smoother and more rounded front end and, although many cars of that era were fitted with rectangular headlights, Karen kept

four round headlights. As was the fashion, the bumpers were now colour-coded and blended in with the main bodyshell, while the top of the wheel arches were more pronounced.

Karen suggested that the main cabin area of the GTE could be retained and that the dashboard could be updated, while still retaining round instruments to capture design features from the original. Naturally such a design would also need a redesigned chassis and a review of the power train.

Middlebridge Scimitar

Although Reliant had now ceased production of the Scimitar GTE and GTC, businessmen John McCauley and Peter Boam believed that there was still a future for it and, after approaching Reliant in 1987, they negotiated a deal whereby they could continue building the Scimitar in small numbers. McCauley and Boam required £400,000 to purchase the design rights to both the Scimitar GTE and GTC, and an estimated £1.5 million to set up production. After meeting with Kohli Nakauchi, President of the Middlebridge group of companies, they were able to buy the manufacturing rights from Reliant and set up Middlebridge Scimitar Ltd in June 1987.

Built by Middlebridge Scimitar Ltd, the Middlebridge Scimitar GTE incorporated more than 450 modifications of the original Reliant design.

While the Middlebridge Scimitar GTE now wore a Middlebridge badge, it still retained the scimitar blade image used in previous sports cars. *Martin North*

Based in Beeston, Nottingham, a new factory was set up and the company made around 450 modifications to the Scimitar SE6b design with a plan to build around three to four cars a week for the executive market. The changes included improved galvanising to the chassis, and enhanced front and rear shock absorbers and springs, while the body benefited from new pearlescence and dual-tone colour paint schemes. The engine was also replaced with a Ford V6 2.9-litre fuel-injection unit with a stainless steel exhaust and a five-speed gearbox. Together with new alloy wheels and redesigned lamp clusters, the interior was given better-quality trim, head restraints and glare-free

A number of completed Middlebridge Scimitar GTEs stand in the Middlebridge premises in Nottingham. *Mick Gaughran*

instruments on the dashboard, while the cars continued to include the usual luxuries like electric windows. The Middlebridge Scimitar works at Lilac Grove were officially opened by HRH The Princess Royal in October 1988, and she ordered a Middlebridge Scimitar that she still owns at the time of writing.

With a price tag of £24,000 (plus extras) the Middlebridge Scimitar GTE was launched at the 1989 Earls Court Motor Fair in London. As per Reliant techniques, the Middlebridge Scimitar was still built by hand with both the chassis and fibreglass bodies continuing to be manufactured by Reliant, then sent on to the Middlebridge factory. Around 100 man hours were spent preparing the body for painting, with an additional 200 man hours on top of that to build each car.

By 1990 changes in the management structure, leading to a reduced workforce, and other issues are said to have affected the company badly. Just thirteen months after its official opening, Middlebridge Scimitar went into receivership after seventy-eight Middlebridge Scimitar GTEs had been built. One Scimitar GTC model was started, but never completed. The production rights to both the Scimitar GTE and GTC were then acquired by Graham Walker Ltd in Chester, Cheshire.

The Middlebridge Scimitar GTE brochure stated that the Scimitar GTE had taken advantage of advances in automotive technology and used an electronic-controlled engine management system.

The fifth Middlebridge Scimitar GTE to be built in 1989 currently belongs to HRH The Princess Royal. *Thomas Touw*

Peeking under the bonnet of a Middlebridge Scimitar GTE reveals a 2.9-litre fuel-injected V6 engine that provides a top speed of more than 140mph (225km/h). *Martin North*

Middlebridge planned to build both the Scimitar GTE and GTC, but only one GTC model was started, and never finished. *Mick Gaughran*

Scimitar SE9

Archive material from Reliant shows that there was a build and development plan for a Scimitar SE9. Drafted in July 1979, it was planned that four prototypes would be developed and built from March 1980, which by coincidence was the date that the Project SE82 was halted.

Prototype 1 would have been right-hand drive and featured a sunshine roof, air conditioning and automatic transmission. This was destined to be built in March 1980 and taken on a 1,000-mile test throughout August and September of that year.

Prototype 2 would have been right-hand drive and fitted with a heater and manual transmission with overdrive. This was due to be built in June 1980 and tested for its performance with a 30,000-mile road endurance.

Prototype 3 was planned to be the same as vehicle 2 but with left-hand drive, and built in August 1980. It would have been subjected to supplier approval tests with a sign-off from Lucas and Girling.

Prototype 4, according to the draft programme, would have been just a chassis and body built in January 1981 and used for seat and anchorage tests.

It was planned that by November 1981 all four vehicles would be signed off by the engineering department and ready for production. Given the plans for the Project SE82 at around the same time and the follow up with the SS1, it can only be assumed that the SE9 project was terminated pretty much as soon as it was drafted. The author enquired about the SE9 with Ritchie Spencer and Ed Osmond, but neither could recall any details of the project.

This rare document suggests the existence of a previously unknown SE9 model, and covers a build and development programme for the SE9 for 1980-81. *Martin North*

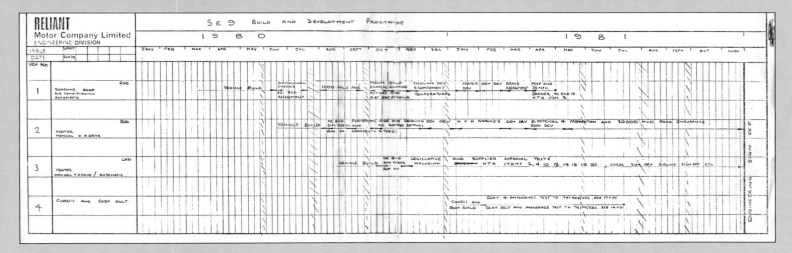

Small Sports go for broke

Cipher

While the GTE was in production, Reliant was well aware that it was beginning to look dated and therefore started to look for a replacement for it. Given the state of the British economy at the time, the company was now considering a car for the small sports car market. Although during the previous year, 1978, Barrie Wills and Ed Osmond's predecessor as Engineering Director, Derek Peck, had rejected an earlier Morgan-like design of his, called the Sienna, Tony Stevens (a freelance designer) designed a second-generation lightweight, open, two-seater sports car that he called the Cipher. Both were based upon a Reliant Kitten chassis and running gear using the Reliant 848cc engine and gearbox. Stevens' Cipher had a tubular steel space-frame mounted to the chassis, which was then covered in separate bolt-on fibreglass panels, a body design that was very reminiscent of the original Lotus Elan.

Reliant built two prototype Stevens Ciphers before ceasing further development, believing that it would be too costly. *Dave Corby*

Derived from a Reliant Kitten, the chassis was heavily modified to create a chassis and space-frame for the Stevens Cipher. *Dave Poole*

Stevens displayed a prototype Cipher at the 1980 Motor Show, where it was well received, although it needed heavy investment to start any kind of production. With this in mind, Stevens approached Ritchie Spencer at Reliant about the possibility of manufacturing the Cipher, and Spencer agreed to build two prototypes for evaluation purposes. Despite the enthusiasm of the workforce who created the prototypes, Reliant worked out that to actually develop the Cipher further to turn it into a production car would cost in excess of £250,000. Stevens did not have sufficient funding and Reliant was not willing to contribute towards it as it had its eye on a Michelotti design (later to become the SS1). Reliant wanted something that could match the performance of the Scimitar GTE, and believed that the Cipher would be underpowered with the 848cc engine, so as a result proceeded no further with the project.

Scimitar SS1

With the potential Scimitar GTE replacement, the SE82 project, terminated, Ritchie Spencer believed that the company now needed to add a small sports car to its line-up. It is rumoured that one possible contender was the Vauxhall Equus concept car, which Reliant was said to have considered making after spotting it at the 1978 Motor Show at the NEC in Birmingham. However, Ritchie Spencer states that he has no knowledge of this at all and adds that

'Our only dealings with Vauxhall were over the name ...

GTE, which we had registered with the SMMT for the Scimitar. These registrations were somewhat of a "Gentlemen's Agreement" rather than being legally binding. Vauxhall paid us a generous sum to allow them to use GTE. This is my only recollection of dealings with Vauxhall/General Motors.'

Reliant's Chief Engineer, Ed Osmond, had previously worked at British Leyland and had been heavily involved with the development of the Triumph TR7. In addition to this he had also worked on a number of prior projects with the Italian car designer Giovanni Michelotti. Although there had been some at Reliant who thought that Michelotti was perhaps past his best, based on his personal experience Osmond drew up a specification for what he believed would be an ideal sports car, then turned to Michelotti to propose a design. Michelotti responded with his first proposal in December 1978, the design itself having a similar profile to that of the TR7. Reliant was considering production when it was approached by Tony Stevens with the Cipher design, as detailed earlier. After turning down Stevens, Ritchie Spencer and the rest of the board approved the Michelotti design and decided to go ahead with it. Unfortunately Michelotti died of cancer in January 1980 before the full finished details were produced. With Michelotti's son, Edgardo, now taking over the Michelotti studios, Reliant decided to continue with the design, which was now being developed further by Michelotti's Japanese designer Tateo Uchida. This was something that Ritchie Spencer believed was unfortunate as, while Uchida is a talented car designer, Spencer felt that he 'did not have the same feel for English-built sports cars that Michelotti did.'

The first Scimitar SS1 prototype, built and registered in July 1983. *Dave Poole*

A side view of the Scimitar SS1 prototype. *Dave Poole*

This rear view of the Scimitar SS1 reveals that it has been badged as a TORA, possibly as a badge styling exercise. *Dave Poole*

The Scimitar SS1 chassis under development. *Dave Poole*

Shortly afterwards, Ed Osmond, now appointed as Engineering Director, proposed a steel backbone chassis for the new sports car. Based upon this, it was decided that rather than use a one-piece bodyshell, the new car could be built using a mix of compression, injection-moulded and SMC press-moulded composite panels (less labour-intensive than their hand-lay counterparts), which could easily be bolted onto the chassis. A large quantity of the major panels (i.e. front and rear sections along with the wings) were made by Dunlop using reinforced injection-moulded plastic. The chassis, manufactured in Germany by Thyssen Nothelfer, which part-funded the tooling, consisted of a basic backbone with welded tubular outriggers attached to a central backbone by triangulated pressed steel plates. The independent rear suspension comprised coil springs and trailing arms (fabricated by Reliant), while up front were double wishbones and coil springs with opposed and inclined telescopic dampers.

It was Ritchie Spencer's intention that the new car would be much cheaper to insure than its predecessors and that it would be available in a number of versions. Initially Reliant considered several possible engines from a number of major manufactures before deciding upon both the Ford 1,300cc and 1,600cc CVH engines, the 1,300 using a four-speed gearbox and the 1,600 a five-speed gearbox. In addition, as

Designed by Ed Osmond, the chassis of the SS1 was a complicated design that used a pressed steel backbone with semi-space-frame outriggers.

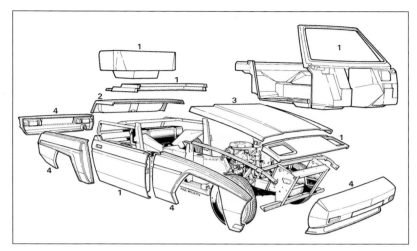

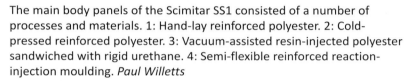

The main body panels of the Scimitar SS1 consisted of a number of processes and materials. 1: Hand-lay reinforced polyester. 2: Cold-pressed reinforced polyester. 3: Vacuum-assisted resin-injected polyester sandwiched with rigid urethane. 4: Semi-flexible reinforced reaction-injection moulding. *Paul Willetts*

The technical cross-section of the Scimitar SS1. *Paul Willetts*

the engines were initially the type used on the Ford Escort, they would help to make the car more appealing to younger buyers. Reliant also intended that at some point the car would also be fitted with a higher-performance engine, so both the chassis and the suspension had been designed to deal with the additional power.

The interior of the car was designed by Reliant designer Jevon Thorpe and used many parts that included Renault switches, Austin Metro stalks and door furniture and a Smiths instrument panel. Taken on by Ed Osmond, Thorpe was serving a placement with Reliant while studying Industrial Design at Lanchester Polytechnic (now Coventry University). Internally, only the cockpit structure, steering wheel and cranked gear cover were manufactured by Reliant. With Reliant outsourcing various body panels to Dunlop, due to their complicated nature, and the chassis to Thyssen Nothelfer, when it came to putting all these together a number of issues had to be faced. Firstly, due to the number of different manufacturing processes of the composite panels, many had different shrinkage tolerances and were therefore not capable of achieving the consistent panel fits and gaps that Reliant specified. Meanwhile the complications involved in creating the chassis meant that each had slightly different dimensions, which again caused issues when attaching components. These issues caused many problems on the assembly line, increasing both operational costs and the time taken to assemble a car. Things were hindered further still when, in 1984, a fire broke out in the Development Department at the Two Gates site. The fire completely destroyed one of the

prototypes and was estimated to have cost Reliant £250,000.

The new car was called the Scimitar SS1 (Small Sports 1), and was launched in both 1,300cc and 1,600cc versions at the 1984 Motor Show at the NEC in Birmingham. Maintaining the idea that it would be a low-cost sports car, it carried a price tag of £7,240 for the 1,300 and just over £8,070 for the 1,600. While the price tag may have

The second Scimitar SS1 prototype was registered in January 1984 as FOH 274V and was written off in 1986 when it overturned at the SCI Road-Going Sports Car Championship.

been favourable, reactions to its looks were much divided, with its over-scalloped panels and varying panel gaps. In addition, Ed Osmond recalls that:

> 'The other interesting thing related to the styling was that the head lamps originally followed the curve of the body and the comment was made by one of the motoring press, when given a preview, that the front of the car looked "sad"... A redesign was carried out fairly late in the development programme to straighten them so that they were horizontal across the car rather than appearing to fall away towards the sides of the car.'

Even with its uncovered rectangular Porsche 928-style pop-up headlights, Ritchie Spencer also admitted that with hindsight the styling at the front of the car was a bit weak and not quite to everyone's taste; as he said,'... the SS1 should have looked prettier; had Michelotti survived, it would have looked better.'

Spencer also acknowledged that Reliant spent far too much on developing the SS1, which ran into millions of pounds.

The SS1 was officially launched in April 1985, although its looks did little to encourage sales. Reliant was already aware that this was, in motoring terms, a small market. In a Christmas letter to all Reliant employees in December 1983, Spencer made the observation that:

> 'Traditionally over 30,000 small sports cars were sold each year in the UK. As many again were sold in Germany and Italy, let alone anywhere else in Europe. Over 100,000 were sold each year in the USA. By world standards in the car industry, this is an insignificant market, which is why the major manufacturers have pulled out. But by our standards the market is huge. Our target is 2,000 units per year; the market sector is there and wide open for us.'

Unfortunately, even 2,000 units per year proved somewhat ambitious, with only 500 units sold in 1985 and 300 the year following. While the 1,300cc version was found to be a bit too slow, offering a top speed of 100mph (160km/h) and a 0-60mph (0-96km/h) of 12.7 seconds, the 1,600cc was marginally better with a top speed of 110mph (179km/h) and a 0-60mph (0-96km/h) time of 9.6 seconds. With standard features including soft velour seats, auxiliary driving lamps, retractable headlamps and a digital clock, optional extras included a removable hard top with a heated rear window, leather trim facings, electric windows and a radio/cassette player.

While retaining the Scimitar name, the small sports cars gained a new badge that still bore the traditional scimitar blade image. *Mark Cropper*

Using pop-up head lamps derived from Triumph TR7 units allowed the Scimitar SS1 to achieve its wedged-shaped nose.

Note in the engine bay of this development Scimitar SS1 the position of the spare wheel ahead of the engine, which followed the trend from earlier Reliant sports cars.

The construction of the SS1 proved to be a major problem for Reliant, which was evident in quality control problems that were said to be costing the company £500,000 a year. In addition, while the vehicle received many criticisms for its looks, there was very little Reliant could actually do about it as the body was made up of numerous expensively tooled panels rather than a single-piece bodyshell, like the Scimitar GTE (the latter allowing more scope for design changes). In addition, with so much of the car being outsourced, long-term contracts had been signed that could not easily be changed or cancelled. Reliant was, therefore, stuck with producing a car that was too expensive to make and, to some observers, somewhat offensive to the eye.

Scimitar 1300/1600/1800Ti

Performance increased dramatically in 1986 when Reliant decided to fit the Nissan Silvia 1800 Turbo engine. This changed the car completely, now giving the SS1 135bhp, a top speed of 126mph (205km/h) and a 0-60mph (0-96km/h) of just 7.6 seconds. Spencer stated that the reason for the delayed introduction of a more powerful SS1, now called the Scimitar 1800Ti, was deliberate, saying that Reliant wanted to establish the SS1 as 'a dream car that most can afford going for volume rather than power first.'

One key benefit that occurred as a result of fitting the Nissan unit was that the emissions were lower, enabling the car to meet USA emissions requirements. Reliant hoped that it would be able to sell around 7,000 extra units per year worldwide and already had a

The nose cones and wings of the Scimitar SS1 were moulded from a rubberised deformable plastic that was able to resist minor impacts.

planned strategy to export the SS1 to the USA; this was apparent during its development, with front and rear bumper sections that complied with US no-damage, low-speed impact requirements (they were made of a reinforced reaction injection-moulded [RRIM] polyurethane designed to recover their original shape after minor impacts).

Fitting the Nissan 1,800cc turbocharged engine to create the Scimitar SS1 1800Ti produced an exceptionally quick sports car, even by today's standards, offering a 0-60mph (0-96km/h) time of around 7.6 seconds.

Following in the tyre tracks of its ancestors, the Scimitar SS1 1800Ti is able to hold its own on the track. One is seen here at Curborough Sprint Course in 2017. *Dave Poole*

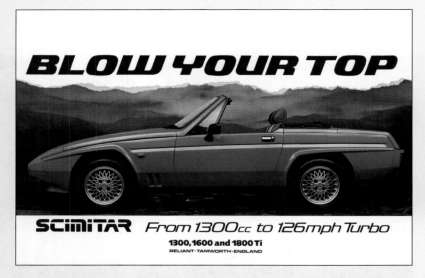

Reliant heavily publicised the open-top virtues of the Scimitar SS1, although this unfortunately did little to boost flagging sales.

Over in Tokyo, Japan, the Scimitar SS1 was viewed as 'the last British light-weight', according to this brochure. *Dave Poole*

The SS1 name was also dropped on the 1,300cc and 1,600cc models, which after a minor facelift became the Scimitar 1300 and Scimitar 1600 respectively. Amongst the changes on the 1800Ti was a black boot spoiler, new alloy wheels and Alcantara seat facing.

While the 1800Ti proved itself to be quite a sportster, such performance came at a price, as the cost of the Nissan engine alone was much higher than the Fords, pushing up the price of the car. By 1986 the Scimitar 1300 cost £7,496, with £8,625 for the 1600 and £10,300 for the 1800Ti. The inclusion of the latter in the range did help to maintain sales for a while, although did little to boost them in the long term, with just 230 sales in 1987, 186 in 1988 and 100 in 1989.

With the 1,300cc engine being phased out by Ford in late 1986, the 1300 model was replaced with the Scimitar SS1 1400 in 1987. *Dave Poole*

Reliant dropped the 1300 model from the range in 1987 and replaced it with the Scimitar 1400, which was powered by a new "Lean Burn" Ford 1,400cc CVH engine. Despite the additional 100cc, on paper the model showed no improvements in performance. While the 1600 and 1800Ti remained essentially the same, an additional optional extra appeared in the form of a roll bar.

Scimitar SS2/Towns' Target

When Cyril Burton, Reliant's Export Director, took over the mantle as Managing Director in April 1987 following Ritchie Spencer's resignation, he soon devised a plan to register 'The Scimitar Motor Company Ltd' as a subsidiary to Reliant and sell it to a third party capable of generating the finance to develop the Scimitar for the North American market. The Universal Motor Group of Companies in the USA was most interested in the Scimitar SS1, so commissioned William Towns (most noted for his designs for Aston Martin) in 1988 to restyle the body for the American market. Based on an 1800Ti and now carrying the moniker SS2, it was given a much more powerful look with much cleaner lines and wider wheel arches. In an October 1989 press release from Reliant, Cyril Burton was quoted as saying:

'Last autumn, we and Universal gave serious consideration to the positioning of the SS2 in the US market in view of the profusion of four-cylinder, lightweight sports cars now coming to the market. Consequently, SS2 is being moved up-market and will be fitted with a new American 3.1-litre V6 engine.

With Ritchie Spencer's resignation in 1987, Cyril Burton took over as Managing Director.

Designed for a possible launch in the USA, the Scimitar SS2 had a much more powerful look with flared wheel arches and cleaner lines.

Taken at the NEC Motor Show in 1988, this shot reveals the rather large and flat rear end of the Scimitar SS2. *Dave Allen*

The front of the Target featured contoured headlamps with integral fog lamps. *Guy Belts*

Developed by William Towns from the Scimitar SS2 concept car, the Target was a set of fibreglass body mouldings designed to fit on a Scimitar SS1 chassis. *Guy Belts*

Reliant do not see this revised US specification as being appropriate for the European market because of restricted servicing facilities and parts availability for the American engine and transmission.'

However, the deal fell through when Universal Motors withdrew funding and the project was abandoned, which resulted in the SS2 design remaining unused. Despite other potential deals, the subsidiary 'Scimitar Motor Company Ltd' was never sold. William Towns then used the SS2 to develop a car called the Target, which was essentially a conversion kit for the Scimitar SS1. An SS1 owner could remove all body panels and replace them with new Target mouldings, which were hand-made in fibreglass. Combined with wider 15-inch wheels, 195/50 low-profile tyres and, if required, a new interior, the completed vehicle had a much more muscular bodyform. The Target conversion retail price, with VAT, was £6,462 plus an additional £999 if a new interior was also required. It is not known whether any conversions were actually sold.

'New' Scimitar/Scimitar SST

William Towns' name soon popped up again in 1989 when Reliant decided to use some elements of the SS2 design in a restyle of the SS1. With Ken Wood heading the development team, the 'New'

Scimitar now used a fibreglass split-monocoque construction sports car body with detachable front and rear bumper mouldings. These helped to give the cars a much cleaner, more modern appearance and instantly had the advantage of making the cockpit more watertight and slightly quieter. For Reliant it also offered huge cost savings as the body could once more be produced in-house, eliminating the higher cost of the outsourced components. Overall quality also benefited as, together with fewer external components, Reliant had full control over body manufacture and could make subtle changes as and when required to ease assembly.

With the 1600 model now dropped from the range, the 1400 and 1800Ti continued to use the Ford CVH 1,400cc and Nissan CA 18ET 1800Ti engines. With a revised chassis that was being promoted as hot-dip galvanised for total corrosion protection, the mechanics on the whole remained the same. Both models had as standard a fold-back soft-top hood, tinted glass, velour seat facings, full-width walnut fascia inserts and cowled, retractable halogen headlamps. Both were also fitted with alloy wheels, the 1400 having a 'smooth style' and the 1800Ti 'spoke-effect' wheels. Optional extras included a hard top with a heated rear window, an opening roof for the hard-top option, a digital stereo radio/cassette, electric windows, a roll bar and metallic paint.

Although displayed at Earls Court in 1989 as the 'New Scimitar 1800Ti', the model was renamed the Scimitar SST shortly afterwards. *Dave Allen*

Derived from the Scimitar SS2 concept, the Scimitar SST used a body that was made entirely of fibreglass, resulting in fewer panel gaps, and body parts that fitted together more accurately.

Even though it had a new body, early Scimitar SST models were criticised for the rather cumbersome-looking black bumper mouldings. *Dave Poole*

The Scimitar SST with its designer William Towns. Later models now featured colour-coordinated bumper mouldings.

The Scimitar SST interior retained many of the features from the Scimitar SS1.

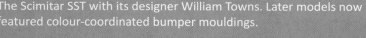

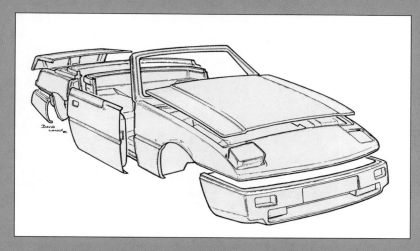

Compared with the Scimitar SS1, the SST used far fewer panels resulting in cleaner lines and more consistency in the build quality. *David Louch*

Headlining Reliant's display at the 1990 Motor Show was this Scimitar SST 1800Ti finished in two-tone metallic silver. *Barry Sidwells*

NEW **SCIMITAR** 1400

POWER BY *Ford*

The initial 1989 brochure for the Scimitar SST only referred to it as the 'New Scimitar'. It wasn't until a reprint in 1991 that the rear of the brochure included the SST moniker.

SCIMITAR

H540 HHJ

Reliant claimed that the 'scorchingly fast' Scimitar SST 1800Ti, with its turbo-injected Nissan engine, was capable of 0-60mph (0-96km/h) in 7 seconds with a top speed of around 130mph (209km/h). *Dave Poole*

When the prototype was exhibited in 1989, it was known simply as the 'New' Scimitar 1400 and the 'New' Scimitar 1800Ti, with an announcement that the car would be available in 1990. The 'New' Scimitar made its first appearance at the SMMT Test 90 at Donnington in May 1990, although the name had now been changed from 'New' Scimitar to the Scimitar SST (the 'T' acknowledging its designer William Towns). In addition, whereas the model displayed in 1989 was shown with colour-coded bumpers, early production models featured black textured bumper mouldings, although these were soon changed for colour-coded ones. Appearing once more at the 1990 Motor Show in Birmingham and badged as the Scimitar SST, the duo were now priced at £11,450 for the Scimitar SST 1400 and £14,100 for the Scimitar SST 1800Ti. Whilst life at Reliant may have looked jolly at the Motor Show, under the bonnet it was starting to break down and just a few months after SST production had started the company was hit by receivership.

The interior of the MGF Concept car bore more than a passing resemblance to that of Reliant's Scimitar SST. *Mark Cropper*

PR2 prototype (MGF Concept car)

In 1990 the Austin Rover Group commissioned three companies to produce a prototype for Austin Rover to evaluate. As part of the project – dubbed Project Phoenix, and codenamed the PR2 prototype (MGF Concept car) by Reliant – each company was given a design brief that detailed the drive train layout and included a fibreglass bodyshell from an earlier concept car called the F-16 with a design attributed to Gerry McGovern. At Reliant, new Chief Engineer Peter Slater was given the brief to produce a front-engine rear-wheel-drive car. Reliant already had

Standing in the corner of the yard at Reliant is one of the PR2/MG shells complete with a Scimitar badge added by a Reliant employee. *Thomas Touw*

The MGF Concept car (PR2 prototype) was created by Reliant for Austin Rover, although the latter chose not to use the design. *Mark Cropper*

its own SS1/SST chassis, so adapted this to fit the bodyshell by elongating the wheelbase and making the track wider, and fitting Austin Maestro front suspension and brakes. The prototype was to use the Rover 3.5-litre fuel-injected V8 engine, so Reliant had to considerably modify the bulkhead so that the engine would fit. Reliant produced and delivered two body moulds and a completed fully working prototype within the 27-week deadline given by Austin Rover, and was the only company to deliver on time. Austin Rover tested and evaluated the PR2 prototype and, while preferring its performance and handling, did not use the Reliant design essentially because it had rear-wheel drive; in the main Austin Rover manufactured front-wheel-drive vehicles and the on-cost of a switch to rear-drive would have proven prohibitive.

Reliant in receivership

Despite many issues throughout its history, Reliant had been able to pick itself up and move forward, although all that was about to change in 1990. During 1983 two property companies (Wiseoak Ltd and Belmont Homes Ltd) had been set up by Carl Turpin and Chris Johnson, and within a few years both companies had become large enough to be floated on the stock market; however, with the housing market boom starting to stall and house prices beginning to fall, both knew that it was not the right time to attempt a flotation. Following a complicated and expensive 'reverse takeover' in February 1990, 37% of Nash Reliant shares were sold to Turpin and Johnson (who both became directors) with Reliant purchasing both building companies for £16.5 million, leaving the housebuilders in control.

Shortly afterwards, Reliant announced that it was going to abandon development work on all new models and instead the main emphasis would be to concentrate on broadening its business operations. The company was so committed to the idea of not being a motor manufacturer that the board asked shareholders' permission to remove the word 'motor' from the company title, to become Reliant Group plc. Their idea then was that the Reliant Group would be relocated to the Kettlebrook site in Tamworth and that the Two Gates site would be torn down and redeveloped as a housing estate by Wiseoak. Theoretically the profits would therefore stay within the group.

Reliant applied for planning permission to redevelop the Two Gates site, then out of nowhere the housing market suddenly crashed, triggering a nationwide recession. Realising that it was now facing serious financial issues, Reliant sold for just £1 the building companies it had recently purchased. In June 1990 the company announced a pre-tax loss of £4.2 million and the debt continued to climb. By September 1990 Reliant's borrowing stood at £5.8 million. Despite every effort and with Reliant Group shares being suspended at an all-time low of £0.03, J. F. Nash Securities Ltd was itself declared insolvent. The receivers were called in at 1.30pm on Thursday 25 October 1990, forcing Reliant to cease trading. Touche Ross was then appointed to handle the affairs of Reliant's motor and industrial divisions and, given Reliant's strong order books, was keen to sell Reliant as a going concern. At the time more than 400 people were employed at the company's Two Gates and Kettlebrook sites, and 115 employees instantly lost their jobs, although the company's then chairman Lord Stokes (formerly Chairman of British Leyland) had pleaded with the bankers to allow Reliant to continue trading.

Among a number of potential buyers was Beans Industries Ltd, which was one of Reliant's largest creditors and as such stood to lose a lot of business if the company collapsed. Beans manufactured the 850cc engine, gearbox, axle and suspension for the Reliant three-wheeler, together with suspension units for the Scimitar. Headed by Lou O'Toole, Beans bought Reliant in July 1991 for an estimated £1.5 million, with vehicle production restarting under its ownership in September 1991. As Beans was located in Tipton, West Midlands, Reliant's offices were moved there, while manufacture of vehicles continued at Tamworth.

Scimitar SST (Beans)

Following Beans' purchase of Reliant, O'Toole was keen to restart production and began building the Scimitar SST again in September 1991, with the same 1400 and 1800Ti models as before. Beans reprinted and reissued Reliant's original 'New' Scimitar flyers, although now the back had been amended to add the letters 'SST', making this a 'New' Scimitar SST 1400 and 1800Ti. While the vehicles themselves remained the same as their pre-receivership counterparts, one difference on the brochure, apart from an address in Tipton, West Midlands, rather than Tamworth, Staffs, was that it now described the Scimitar SST as being compatible for both leaded and unleaded fuel. Building cars was not seen as an issue for Beans. The former Jaguar superintendent O'Toole reported in an October 1991 press release that:

> 'Many of our management at Beans have first-hand experience of the car industry... You'll see very finely engineered, built and finished vehicles coming out of Reliant.'

Sabre (Beans)

Under Beans' ownership, Reliant was keen to create a new sports car and came up with a new model within six weeks. It is worth noting here that given Reliant's plans to abandon all future vehicle development in February 1990 and move away from being a vehicle manufacturer, if it had not have gone into liquidation later that year all future sports models would have ceased there and then.

Re-introducing a name from Reliant's sporting past, the Sabre 1800 was launched in July 1992. *Dave Poole*

Scimitar Sabre (Beans)

Delving into the drawer marked 'History', it was decided to bring back a name from Reliant's past, the Sabre. Using the SST 1800Ti as a base, the bodywork was developed further by incorporating smoother lines, colour-coded bumpers and boot spoiler, larger 15-inch five-spoke alloy wheels and flared wheel arches. It included electric windows, electric mirrors, a stereo radio cassette, and leather upholstery as standard. Both the roll bar and a hard top continued as optional extras.

A prototype was completed in 1991 and unveiled at the Earls Court Motor Show in October of that year, where it created a great deal of interest. While the Sabre had used the 1800 Nissan turbocharged engine, its 1,400cc counterpart remained a Scimitar SST 1400 and was sold alongside. With a price tag of £14,900, the Sabre 1800 was launched in July 1992 and was well received by both the press and purchasers alike due to its improved build quality and excellent performance, maintaining its predecessor's top speed of 126mph (203km/h) and a 0-60mph (0-96km/h) time of just 7.6 seconds.

O'Toole was well aware of which vehicles were bringing money into Reliant, and in the September 1992 edition of *Autocar & Motor* he was quoted as saying:

> 'The three-wheeler is our bread and butter while Sabre and Scimitar are our jam and cream. I can drop them and increase three-wheeler build if I want to.'

The jam and cream, however, were starting to go sour as sales of the small sports continued to decline. Stewart Halstead, Reliant's Sales Director, came up with the idea of a new model that he hoped would 'recoup some of the massive investment in the SS project', and this became the Scimitar Sabre 1400. It incorporated what Reliant termed the new more 'muscular' body shape that was being used on the Sabre 1800. It also sported new Compomotive 14-inch alloy wheels with Bridgestone 185/60/R14 tyres and colour-coded bumpers. Due to the vast amount of component stock Beans held, the company was able to cut the retail price and offer the Scimitar

Sabre 1400 at £11,900. This was deemed to be the lowest-priced British-built sports car with full national type approval available in the UK at that time, the price tag being around £3,000 less than its nearest competitor, the Mazda MX5.

Reliant was keen to develop the sports car side of the business and, to a certain degree, segregate the Scimitar and the Sabre as a separate 'Scimitar Sports Cars' division. This was most notable in October 1992 when, at the Motor Show at the NEC, the Reliant three-wheelers were branded under Reliant while the announcement of the new Scimitar Sabre 1400 came under the Scimitar Sports Cars brand. Powered by the Ford 1400 CVH engine, the Scimitar Sabre 1400 was launched in 1993.

For many sporting Reliant enthusiasts the 1990s represents a challenging time in identifying certain features of a vehicle, as it appears that Reliant made various changes and 'mixed and matched' various parts to help complete a vehicle. Some vehicles sported different components, such as front and rear bumpers for example, which suggested the possibility of a Sabre Mk 1.5 to some. Others, however, believe that the Mk 1.5 designation is not actually a specific model and essentially just appears to include certain vehicles that are a mix of both Scimitar SST and Sabre parts.

Project R931

With the Scimitar and Sabre models finding it increasingly tougher to compete with other cars on the market, Lou O'Toole was keen to develop a new 'baby' sports car. With a planned price tag of less than £10,000, it would lower the cost of sports car ownership and, in Reliant's words, make it a reality for more drivers.

Before the 1992 Motor Show there was much media speculation that Reliant (or Scimitar Sports Cars as it was being advertised) was going to unveil a new sports coupé that was going to be based on the Reliant Fox chassis (the Fox being a four-wheeled utility vehicle from Reliant's economy range). As a result, visitors at the show went over to the Reliant stand full of

Top: The proposed baby sports car design (Project R931) was unveiled at the 1992 Motor Show and received very mixed reviews from those who saw it.

Middle and bottom: Side views of the baby sports car showing both soft top and coupé models. *Giles Chapman Library*

When Reliant announced in 1992 that it was producing a 'baby sports car', *Autocar & Motor* magazine ran an article on Reliant's plans. Although it had no images of the proposed car, Iain Robertson at *Autocar* imagined this design of how the new Reliant might look, based upon the sparse details that Reliant had provided. *Autocar*

111

anticipation to see the new car ... and instead were treated to an information pack and a questionnaire on a new baby sports car codenamed Project R931. On show were visuals of the proposed car and visitors were asked questions about the specifications, which, it was said, would help Reliant to decide whether such a car should be put into production at a planned 2,000 vehicles a year.

The design element of R931 was being handled by Fergus Engineering, and the initial plans for the car were that it would be a two-seater, rear-wheel-drive design available as either a convertible or a coupé. Reliant was going to use a semi-monocoque steel chassis fitted with a multi-point, fuel-injection catalysed version of its all-alloy 848cc engine. This, they estimated, would be capable of around 95mph (153km/h) with a 0-60mph (0-96km/h) time of around 11.5 seconds.

The body concept was based on an original design by Lester Allen Associates and would have used thermoplastic panels. The initial reaction to R931 was said to have been 'strong', although opinions on the new design were very much divided, with some believing the best place for the plans was in the bin. Whatever the aim, Reliant was soon hit with another receivership and consequently the project came to a halt.

Scimitar Sabre Mk II (Beans)

The Scimitar Sabre with its Ford 1400 engine proved to be rather underpowered and sales continued to decline. Stewart Halstead recalls that by 1993:

'...sales of SS around this time were non-existent. Via Beans Industries, the then owners of Reliant, we had access to Rover's range of engines at a good price and hence with a bit of mould development we produced the Scimitar Sabre and engineered in the 1.4 K series engine.'

The result was a new model, dubbed by some as the Scimitar Sabre Mk II, which now used a Rover 1.4 K series 16-valve engine and featured further enhancements that included restyled front bumper and lamps. It created considerable European market interest when it was exhibited at the 1994 Geneva Motor Show. Halstead notes that eighteen cars were sold 'straight off the stand'.

A few months later, in October that year, the Scimitar Sabre was again on display at the Birmingham Motor Show. In addition to the 1400, a prototype 2-litre version was displayed, powered by a Rover 2.0 T series 16-valve engine. However, the engine was considered too heavy, so while it was featured in at least one Reliant brochure no production models with the 2-litre engine were built. Stewart Halstead confirms this:

'...we built one development car and it may well have been built in Blackpool at the engineering area of TVR ... it was thought that the 2-litre engine was too heavy.'

The idea of the 2-litre version was therefore dropped with no further development.

Above: Exhibited at the 1994 Birmingham Motor Show, the Scimitar Sabre 2.0 remained a one-off. *John Hawthorn*

Right: This was the only Reliant brochure that displayed information on both the Scimitar Sabre 1.4 and the Scimitar Sabre 2.0, although it provided no performance figures.

Above: Both flavours of the Scimitar Sabre, with the soft-top and hard-top options – a Scimitar Sabre 1800Ti is on the left and a Scimitar Sabre 1400 on the right. *Dave Poole*

With the Scimitar Sabre the style and shape of the small sports had become much neater and more desirable, although competing against cars like the Mazda MX was now making sales much tougher for Reliant.

Believed by some to be a development model, this particular 1994 Sabre was actually a one-off, built independently by a former employee while at Reliant. *Dave Poole*

A Scimitar Sabre at Reliant in 1994, sporting a Rover 1.4-litre K series engine. *Barry Sidwells*

In the same year a restyled Sabre was built at Reliant, which over the years was believed by some to be a development model to replace the Sabre from 1995. However, the vehicle was never intended for production and was actually a one-off built independently by a former employee using a mixture of components from various parts bins.

Unfortunately Reliant was soon due to be hit by another blow. Due to debts with some of its subsidiaries and, in particular, one major customer withholding a payment of £100,000, Beans went in to receivership in November 1994 with debts of around £2 million, taking Reliant with it. Even though Reliant was once again up for sale, it was able to continue production at a rate of fifteen three-wheelers and five Scimitar Sabres a week. By December 1994 this had dropped to eight three-wheelers and one Scimitar Sabre each week, due to a further slump in sales.

Unlike when the Scimitar GTE was at its peak and assembled on an assembly track, it is apparent from this photo that both built and half-built vehicles are occupying the same floor space. *Barry Sidwells*

The Scimitar Sabre assembly shop at Reliant in 1994. *Barry Sidwells*

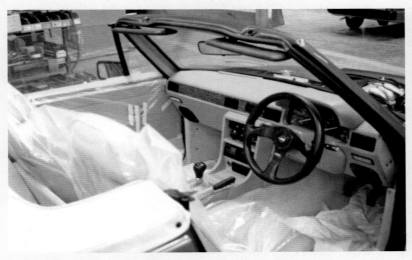 

Freshly assembled, the whole interior is protected by plastic to avoid any marks before the vehicle reaches the dealers. *Barry Sidwells*

Another view of the Scimitar Sabre assembly shop in 1994. *Barry Sidwells*

Scimitar Sabre Mk II (Avonex)

In January 1995 Reliant was sold to the Avonex Group Ltd as a going concern, while the land at the Two Gates site was sold to Tamworth-based property developer Smiths Brothers. Avonex therefore continued to manufacture cars at Two Gates while leasing the land from Smiths Brothers. The Avonex takeover was led by Peter Hall who, when asked by the *Tamworth Trader* newspaper if Reliant would stay in Tamworth for the foreseeable future, replied:

'Of course it will. Reliant and Tamworth go together like Ferrari and Italy. This company helped put Tamworth on the map.'

Unfortunately, Avonex didn't have Ferrari's bank balance and, with limited funds remaining and a workforce of just thirty employees, Reliant continued three-

wheeler production together with the Scimitar Sabre, although by now production of the latter had been cut back to just one car a week.

Peter Hall, in charge at Reliant when it was acquired by the Avonex Group Ltd, is seen here as production of the Scimitar Sabre commenced.

115

Manufactured in 1995, this particular Scimitar Sabre 1400 would have been among the last of the Scimitar Sabres to roll off the production line at Reliant. *Thomas Touw*

Retaining the same recipe as its Beans incarnation, production of the Scimitar Sabre was to be hit again just a few months later in October 1995. With huge debts mounting, Avonex itself fell into financial difficulty and the 'For Sale' sign was up again at Reliant. As a result production of the Scimitar Sabre ceased and it remained the last sports car to be built by Reliant, although there were a number of further attempts to resurrect the Scimitar name.

Proposed Scimitar replacements (Heynes)

In March 1996 Reliant was sold to Jonathan Heynes, the son of Jaguar's former Vice Chairman William M. Heynes, and shortly afterwards ownership was split three ways between entrepreneur

Kevin Leech, Burton West Ltd (part of San Engineering & Locomotive Co Ltd of India) and Heynes. An agreement was reached that while Heynes would take day-to-day control and run the business, cash needs would be met equally from the three sources. With the sale concluded, the company name was changed to Reliant Cars Ltd. Under Jonathan Heynes, Reliant's main emphasis initially was to get the three-wheeled Robin back into full production, which in turn would bring the cash flowing in. This was achieved in less than six months.

Heynes was also keen to get the Sabre back into production, although there was a problem, as Heynes recalls:

'The key chassis tooling and some body moulds for the Sabre had "disappeared" via the administrators during early 1996 and with the time and cash needed to resurrect the Sabre we believed a new car should be developed.'

Based on the shell from the PR2 project, this was a design created by Cliff Ruddell in January 1997 as a possible Scimitar replacement. *Jonathan Heynes*

Scimitar GTE

Leech and Heynes were interested in creating a new Scimitar that was based on the original Scimitar GTE concept. When Heynes took over Reliant a prototype MG body was acquired that had become redundant from the PR2 project for the MGF Concept car (see page 108). A senior Jaguar consultant, Cliff Ruddell, took details and photos of the MGF body prototype and, using the measurements and general scheme, styled an open-topped version.

Another concept was also created by newly established Clayton Hamilton Automotive Design in Essex, which presented a sleek-looking Scimitar GTE design that was based around a Rover V8 car the company had developed. Heynes showed the various styles to Leech and says that:

> '...he was very enthusiastic and allocated £25,000 (outside the shareholders' investment agreement) to produce more details and a body... [It] seems a low figure these days but we could have produced a full GRP body prototype as we had retained the in-house skills.'

Top right: This design for a new Scimitar GTE in 1997 would, if produced, have brought back a large Scimitar to the market. *Jonathan Heynes*

Right: The rear of the proposed Scimitar GTE incorporated a rear hatch and rising waistline as in the original. *Jonathan Heynes*

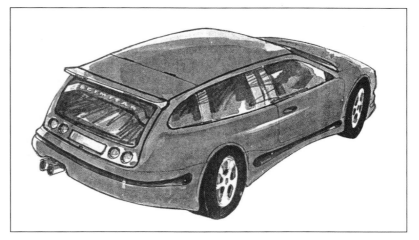

With its Scimitar GTE design not used by Reliant, Clayton Hamilton Automotive Design used styling cues from it to create the CHAD Super Sport 4. With a galvanised chassis and fibreglass body, it was almost a coupé version of the proposed GTE concept.

It was believed that the chassis and suspension from the original Scimitar GTE could be modified, as Reliant had spares for the chassis in stores and available via Graham Walker Ltd; however, this may have raised the question of licensing with Middlebridge.

Unsure about the availability of the Ford V6 engines, Reliant had built up a good relationship with Nissan, so it was possible that the new GTE could be Nissan-powered. However, despite the interest in producing a larger GTE alternative, plans were halted and, instead, Reliant decided to replace the Sabre with another small sports model.

The last Scimitar

Reliant decided to replace the Sabre with a car that was designed by Geoff Wardle and engineering consultant Tom Bishop. Work began on a small two-seater with a fibreglass body, and featuring a large front grille that it was proposed would close to reduce drag. Moreover, it would also have a shaped windscreen that curved around the driver and passenger while dipping in the centre. Both Wardle and Bishop were quite adventurous, so wanted to make an impact with novel features like a moving windscreen and T-shaped top panels. It was planned that the windscreen would be height-

adjustable via a mechanical screw, so when it was in the lowered position it would have a look reminiscent of twin Brooklands aero-screens. This would have been combined with a conventional folding hood as on earlier Reliant vehicles, although a concept was also suggested where a folding roof was fitted.

Designed by Geoff Wardle and Tim Bishop, this new small Scimitar design was approved for development. *Jonathan Heynes*

One of the unique features of the new Scimitar was a large front grille, which, it was proposed, would close to reduce drag. *Jonathan Heynes*

Another feature on the new Scimitar was a height-adjustable windscreen that could be lowered to give a Brooklands effect. *Jonathan Heynes*

Reliant was also testing an EFI MPI version of the standard 848cc Reliant engine (from Reliant's economy models) that used fuel injection and was being developed in-house by Bishop. It was envisaged that this engine would be fitted in the new Scimitar, and was to be placed further back in the chassis, well behind the front wheels, driving the rear wheels via a Honda six-speed gearbox. Combined with a lightweight chassis and body, this would have produced around 70bhp. The chassis would have been made from tubular steel with McPherson struts and a live rear axle with a conventional braking system sourced from MG. In addition to the Reliant engine, given the company's relationship with Nissan, a Nissan 1,000cc alloy engine was also considered.

Speaking of Kevin Leech, Jonathan Heynes notes that he:

'...was a remarkable businessman, and "took to Reliant" and personally created enthusiasm. He was of course careful with his funding, which was controlled by an accounting team in Jersey... Kevin at the time was controlling some sixty companies worldwide and obviously was a busy man, and left me to run Reliant my way. I have no doubt his heart was in Reliant and he personally took interest in the sports car programme.'

Both Heynes and the other investor, San Engineering & Locomotive Co Ltd in India, matched Leech's funding pound for pound. However, an issue arose in 1998 when the investors were informed that Reliant would be leaving its ancestral Tamworth site and relocate to the Fletcher speed boat company in Burntwood, Staffordshire. This was as a result of Leech's Glen Investment Company having purchased Fletcher speed boats. San Engineering was somewhat jittery about the move and as a result sold its shares to Leech, which resulted in him taking control of Reliant. Heynes also wanted to stay

The proposed interior of the new Scimitar. *Jonathan Heynes*

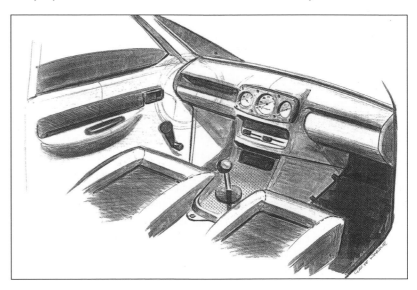

in Tamworth and purchase the Two Gates site that Reliant was then leasing. Talking of the impact this had, Heynes comments that:

'This caused a ripple and accountants took a closer look. The senior accountant, an aggressive man, was very much against Kevin Leech's further funding of Reliant and showed no interest in the future of a sports car. With that the extra funding stopped, the allocated funding went to Fletcher. We had little choice but to stop the sports car prototype work.'

Built by San Motors, both the San Storm (seen here) and the saloon version, the San Streak, were for a short while models offered by Reliant.

Created by Geoff Wardle, if finished this would have been a full-scale model of a new Scimitar. It was 75% completed before the project was terminated and the model destroyed. Note the shape of the windscreen outline, ready to be cut out. *Andy Plumb*

Heynes was requested to stop further engineering work and to abandon all projects, including the new Scimitar. By now a full-size scale model of the new car had been constructed by Wardle. Made of high-density foam, it was 75% complete before the decision was made to abandon it. Instead, all emphasis was now back on restyling the three-wheeled Robin, the exterior of which designer Andy Plumb had modified and Heynes had signed off. The move to the Fletcher site was inevitable as the accountants envisaged boats and cars together in one factory. While the Robin bravely soldiered on, the possibilities of a new Reliant sports car had by then all but vanished. Heynes believes that:

> 'The initial proposals to reintroduce the Scimitar brand were logical and we had a good engineering team hard at work. We were regretfully caught out by an accountant who did not have the vision to progress and support us with the sports car programme.'

Heynes decided to leave Reliant, selling his shares ratio to Leech. In December 1998 the Tamworth site closed its doors for the final time and moved to Burntwood, some 15 miles away.

San Storm

Prior to Jonathan Heynes' departure in 1998, Reliant had been distributing advertising material for a small sports car called the San Storm, together with a saloon model called the San Streak. The vehicles were built by San Motors India Ltd (a division of Reliant's shareholders San Engineering & Locomotive Co Ltd) and were planned to be made available in the UK through Reliant. As with Reliant's sports cars, the San Storm was an open-top two-seater with a fibreglass body. It was powered by a Renault D7F 1,149cc fuel-injected engine that, combined with the car's low kerb weight of 650kg, delivered 60bhp to provide a top speed of 100mph (160km/h) and a 0-62mph (0-100km/h) time of 11 seconds. Well-equipped with air conditioning, electric windows and alloy wheels, the car's potential link to Reliant was soon dropped when, in the same year, San Engineering sold their shares to Kevin Leech.

A Scimitar for the millennium

In December 2000 *Auto Express* magazine claimed a world exclusive, stating that Reliant was bringing back the Scimitar name with a new sports car. Norman Whitaker, in charge of sales at that time, was said to have informed the magazine that Reliant's owner, Kevin Leech, had purchased the manufacturing rights for the De la Chapelle Roadster manufactured in France. Reliant would build the roadster and rebadge it as a Scimitar. Using a tubular steel space-frame clad with a fibreglass body, the car was powered by a Peugeot engine that, in the more powerful model, provided a 0-60mph (0-96km/h) time of 6 seconds and a top speed of around 140mph (225km/h).

Rebadged as a Reliant Scimitar, the De la Chapelle Roadster was planned to reignite the Scimitar name, although unforeseen financial events behind the scenes prevented it from happening. *Xavier de la Chapelle*

Had plans been successful, the De la Chapelle Roadster in its Scimitar form would have taken the Scimitar brand into the new millennium. *Xavier de la Chapelle*

Xavier de la Chapelle recalls that:

'We had a lot of discussions with Reliant at that time, we signed an NDA, they sent a test pilot from McLaren F1 to test the Roadster in France and he was delighted by the road holding and the quality of the car.'

It was envisaged that the Scimitar version would have had a variety of engines from 2 litres up to a 3-litre V6. Furthermore, the standard model would be fitted with a soft top, with the option of a metal roof also available. With electric windows, aluminium pedals and a flush-fitting tonneau cover among the standard features, the Scimitar was expected to go on sale in late spring 2001 at a retail price ranging from £18,000 to £23,000.

Contrary to the *Auto Express* report, de la Chapelle reveals that, while Reliant did plan to purchase the manufacturing rights, it did not actually go through with it and the new Scimitar did not go ahead. De la Chapelle was informed that Reliant's main shareholder was facing 'big financial problems in 2000 due to his investments in internet companies'.

Reliant had continued to make the three-wheeled Robin, although in September 2000 it announced that production was going to end, the last three-wheeler leaving the production line on 14 February 2001. With the dotcom bubble bursting in October 2002, Kevin Leech became bankrupt virtually overnight as his investments collapsed. Reliant then ceased trading and its subsidiary, Reliant PartsWorld, was passed over to Stewart Halstead, who then moved the operation to Cannock in Staffordshire. Headed by Halstead and Adrian Pearson, the company offers replacement parts and reconditioned engines for Reliant economy vehicles.

After Reliant moved from Tamworth to Cannock, it was soon announced that the old premises would be torn down and replaced by a new housing estate named 'Scimitar Park'. Sadly for Scimitar enthusiasts, the name remains invisible as none of the street names in the new estate acknowledged the sports car range, instead all being named after the company's cofounder and economy models. *Barry Sidwells*

While a new housing estate may now sit on the old Reliant ground, Reliant vehicles can occasionally still be seen as enthusiasts take vehicles back for a nostalgic photo, as here with a 1969 Scimitar GTE in Tom Williams Way. *Dave Poole*

Graham Walker Ltd

Based in Chester, UK, Graham Walker Ltd has been a family-run car business for almost fifty years. Specialising in the Reliant Scimitar, among many other marques, Graham Walker was instrumental in assisting Middlebridge with the Middlebridge Scimitar and indeed became the first Middlebridge Scimitar dealer.

In 2014 the production and brand rights for the Scimitar GTE and GTC were acquired by Graham Walker Ltd, which now owns many of the moulds and tooling. To date, the company has been able to officially restore or make new Scimitars to order identical to those that left the Reliant factory throughout the 1960s and '70s, although inflation has increased the prices somewhat from that era.

Appendix 1
Reliant sports car code names

All sports cars at Reliant received an 'SE' code name, derived from the first and last letter of the name Sabre. This differs from Reliant's economy and export four-wheelers, which were given an 'FW' (Four-Wheeler) code name.

SE1	Sabre Four
SE2	Sabre Six
SE3	Sabre V8 (V8 powered; abandoned)
SE4	Scimitar GT (straight six coupé)
SE4a	Scimitar GT (3-litre V6 coupé)
SE4b	Scimitar GT (improved interior)
SE4c	Scimitar GT (2.5-litre V6 coupé)
SE5	Scimitar GTE (3-litre)
SE5a	Scimitar GTE (uprated)
SE6	Scimitar GTE (enlarged to 3-litre)
SE6a	Scimitar GTE (improved)
SE6b	Scimitar GTE (2.8-litre)
SE7	Scimitar GTE (four-door version [FW11]; abandoned)
SE8	Scimitar GTC prototype (3-litre)
SE8b	Scimitar GTC (2.8-litre)
SE82	Scimitar GTE (replacement prototype; abandoned)
SE9	Scimitar GTE (abandoned)
SS1	Scimitar SS1 (small two-seater 1.3-litre and 1.6-litre)
1800ti	Scimitar 1800Ti (Nissan turbo engine)
SS2	Scimitar SS2 (Concept car)
SST	Scimitar SST

Models with no codename, 1990 onwards

Sabre	Sabre
Scimitar Sabre	Scimitar Sabre (Ford and Nissan engine)
Scimitar Sabre Mk II	Scimitar Sabre (Rover and Nissan engine)

Other potential sports models

FW6	Rebel 1600 GT (prototype)
FW7	Mid-engined two-seater (prototype)
FW8	Bond Equipe replacement (abandoned project)
FW11	Potential Anadol replacement and later SE7 (abandoned)
PR2	MGF Concept car (prototype)
R931	Baby Sports car (No development)

Appendix 2
Sports car production figures

Sabra	333
Sabre	44
Sabre Six	77
Scimitar GT SE4 (straight six)	297
Scimitar GT SE4a (3-litre V6)	539
Scimitar GT SE4b (3-litre V6)	51
Scimitar GT SE4C (2.5-litre V6)	118
Scimitar GTE SE5	2,469
Scimitar GTE SE5a	6,635
Scimitar GTE SE6	543
Scimitar GTE SE6a	3,877
Scimitar GTE SE6b	437
Scimitar GTC SE8b	442
Scimitar SS1 (various engines)	1,507
Scimitar SST	45
Sabre Mk 1	39
Sabre Mk 1.5 (seems to have been a mix of SST and Sabre parts)	20
'Scimitar' Sabre Mk 2	100*
Middlebridge Scimitar GTE	79
Middlebridge GTC	1
Approximate total of Reliant sports cars	17,203

* 91 built, 9 unfinished/unregistered

Appendix 3
Reliant sports car related clubs

Reliant Motor Club

Formed in April 2016 by Reliant enthusiast Elvis Payne and Mark Cropper, the Reliant Motor Club (RMC) offers members a large online archive full of historical information for not only sporting Reliant enthusiasts/owners but also for the economy vehicles. The club is delighted to have HRH The Princess Royal as a honorary member and Barrie Wills, the club's President, who was appointed to the board of directors at Reliant in February 1974. In addition to being one of the co-founders, the author is also the Chairman and the Historian for the club.

Together with brochures, price lists, press releases and numerous other documents, the online archive also includes every copy of the Reliant Review (Reliant's in-house publication) from 1963 to 1977.

For more information visit: http://www.reliant.website

Reliant Owners Club

The Reliant Owners Club (ROC) was founded in London 1958. The club is open to all Reliant Owners and enthusiast. The ROC holds social meetings throughout the year as well as car meets, road runs, and a yearly weekend camping weekend/rally.

For more information visit: www.reliantownersclub.com

Reliant Sabre & Scimitar Owners Club

The RSSOC caters for all Reliant sports cars, from the company's first true sports car, the Reliant Sabre, through to the later Scimitar Sabre produced towards the end of Reliant's history. Although fewer than 400 of the early cars were built and few exist today, the Sabre was the prime reason for the existence of the Club in 1972.

For more information visit: http://www.scimitarweb.co.uk

Bibliography

Auto Express magazine: December 2000

Autocar magazine: various editions

Birmingham Post: 1970

Dave Poole's 'Sporting Reliants' website at
    www.sportingreliants.com

Reliant brochures and publications: various, 1955-95

Reliant internal documents: various, 1975-90

Reliant Review: various editions, 1963-77

Reliant Review: various editions, 1996-98

Rebel without Applause (Daniel Lockton, 2003)

Tom Karen: The Man from Ogle (DVD, RSSOC, 2016)

Tamworth Herald: various editions, 1961-98

Tamworth Trader: various editions, 1995

The Reliant Motor Company (Elvis Payne, 2016)

The Scimitar and its Forebears (Don Pither, 2nd ed, 1990

Websites for further information on Reliant sports cars

(all available at time of publication)

Dave Poole's 'Sporting Reliants' website: www.sportingreliants.com

Graham Walker: www.grahamwalkerltd.co.uk

Middlebridge Scimitar: www.middlebridge-scimitar.co.uk

Reliant Motor Club: www.reliant.website

Reliant Owners Club: www.reliantownersclub.com

Reliant PartsWorld: www.reliantpartsworld.co.uk

Reliant Sabre & Scimitar Owners Club: www.scimitarweb.co.uk

Index